DELECTABLE
ITALIAN DISHES
for family and friends

DELECTABLE ITALIAN DISHES

for family and friends

Sal Baldanza

Kerriann Flanagan Brosky

Maple Hill Press

Back cover photo by Tom Decker.

All food photographs by Kerriann Flanagan Brosky.

Family photographs courtesy of the Baldanza and Flanagan families.

Website: www.delectableitaliandishes.com

ISBN 978-0930545-27-7

Printed in Singapore

*Sooner or later, we must realize
there is no station,
no one place to arrive at
once and for all.*

The true joy of life is in the trip.

— Robert J. Hastings

Table of Contents

Pizza, Breads & Paninis

Pasta

Seafood

Poultry

Dedication

I dedicate this cookbook, in loving memory, to my father Francesco Baldanza, and to my two sisters Anna and Franca Baldanza. I dedicate this to my two beautiful children as well, in the hope that they will be as fortunate as I to discover a passion in life as fulfilling as I have found in my love for food, family, and friends.

— Sal Baldanza

I'd like to dedicate this book to the person from whom I inherited my love and appreciation of food ... my mother, Deanna Flanagan. She not only taught me how to cook, but she was the true inspiration for writing this book. Thank you for sharing so many of your wonderful recipes with me, and for always believing in my work.

— Kerriann Flanagan Brosky

Acknowledgments

First I'd like to acknowledge my mother, Aida Baldanza, as she taught me a love of food and continues to be a source of inspiration. I'd like to thank my brothers Alberto, Rocco, and Joe Baldanza for their constant partnership, love, and contributions that have made it possible in many ways for me to do this book. A special thanks to my nephew Frankie, who helped me compile some of the recipes.

I'd especially like to thank my wife, Kate. I am very lucky to have found her when I came to this country. She is smart, beautiful, a great mother to our two children, and a pretty good cook too! I couldn't have completed my work for this book without her.

— Sal

I'd like to thank Jenny Studenroth for the many years she has dedicated herself to organizing my office and my projects, and for the hours she has spent going through the more than 1000 photographs I initially took for this book. Your work has been invaluable.

To my neighbors and friends, Marijo and Mario Giammarino, for being "the taste kitchen" for this project. There was many a night when I'd run a new dish across the street for you to try. It's great sharing a love of food with you.

To Joe Tursi, my Italian instructor, for his patience in teaching me this beautiful language and for making learning such fun. You've enabled me to speak to the Baldanzas in their own tongue, however simple my attempts may be.

To Joseph Crocilla for always making me look good, and for sharing your love of Italian food and the Italian language with me. It's always great to practice speaking with you.

To my uncle, Darryl Ellis, for his work in restoring the wonderful photos of my grandfather that appear in this book. Thanks for helping to keep his memory alive.

To my publisher, Julie, for always believing in my work, and for the countless hours she has spent on all my books throughout the years. Your friendship is one I will forever treasure.

To my beautiful sons, Ryan and Patrick, for trying and loving everything I make. You are already food connoisseurs. I treasure my time cooking with you in the kitchen.

To my husband, Karl, who encouraged both Sal and me to pursue this project. For his love, support and guidance during the many late nights he spent assisting me in the kitchen, during photo shoots or in designing recipe templates on the computer. I am so fortunate and grateful to have you in my life. I could not have completed this project without you. Thank you for believing in me.

— Kerriann

FOREWORD

When Sal Baldanza and I set out to create this cookbook, we wanted it to be a personal expression of our lives, our families and our love of cooking. It's one thing to put recipes on a page; it's another thing to delve into the passion behind them. Along with 100 recipes, we have included two brief "backstories" at the end of the book to give you glimpses of our very different family histories and how they helped to shape our lives and our shared love of delicious, fresh food.

The first story tells of Sal's journey to this country, his struggles and sacrifices to create a business and to succeed at it. For those of you who know the very popular pork and Italian specialty store called Mr. Sausage, here is the long-awaited tale of how it all came to be.

As for me — an author, photographer, and "ghost buster" — I have provided insight into another side of my life … a love of cooking and the friendships I have made with the Baldanzas because of it. When Sal and I were children, our respective families introduced us to wonderful foods and to cooking, and we'd like to share these experiences with you.

We thought long and hard about what recipes to include in this book. Some are traditional, while others spin a new twist on modern Italian cooking. Many of the recipes have been influenced by our mothers, both wonderful Italian cooks. Sal and I divided the project up equally, and in most cases have not distinguished which recipes are whose.

Italian cooking is relatively easy and fun. I hear from so many people that cooking is too difficult or time-consuming, but it doesn't have to be. Anyone can cook our recipes. However, we do recommend using the freshest of ingredients, and urge you not to substitute any ingredient unless it is suggested. Another important element for success is to use fresh herbs whenever possible. Most of our recipes call for fresh herbs, so don't use dried herbs unless the recipe specifically calls for them (which is rare). These days fresh herbs are easy to find at the store — and you can even grow them on a windowsill or in a small garden. Take advantage of them; they will make a huge difference in your cooking!

The other advice we offer is to let cooking come naturally. We have given exact measurements for all the ingredients, but after you have tried a recipe, we recommend experimenting by using the measurements as a guideline. A tablespoon or two more in a sauté pan won't spoil anything, and it may make a difference in your enjoyment of a dish. Where wine is concerned, use your judgment. If a recipe calls for a cup of wine, you can take out your measuring cup and get it just right, but we'd rather see you pour it in directly from the bottle. Be adventurous! You'll enjoy cooking much more if you let things flow naturally. This is how we both learned to cook. Once you get used to being a cook (or if you already are), you'll no longer need to follow the measurements exactly. You'll get a "feel" for cooking through taste, smell, sight and texture. The only time exact measurements are really necessary is in baking.

This book offers quick and easy every-night meals, as well as some delicious, more involved dishes you can make for entertaining. So put on some good Italian music and open a bottle of wine. Pour yourself a glass, and then save the rest for cooking. Cook like the Italians do … just relax and enjoy. Mangiamo!

— *Kerriann Flanagan Brosky*

APPETIZERS

Antipasti

Crostini with Three Pesto

Crostini con Tre Pesto

This pesto can also be served over ravioli or tortellini as a main pasta dish.

Ingredients

1 bunch fresh basil
4 cups baby spinach
4 cups baby arugula
6 cloves garlic, chopped
1 cup crumbled gorgonzola cheese
1 cup lightly toasted walnuts
⅓ cup extra virgin olive oil
salt and pepper to taste
1 long baguette

Instructions

Preheat oven to 350°. Place all ingredients except the olive oil in a food processor, and process on high for several minutes until finely chopped. Slowly add olive oil until incorporated, and consistency is a smooth paste.

Slice baguette into ¼-inch slices and brush with olive oil. Toast on a cookie sheet for 3-5 minutes. Spread pesto on toasted crostini rounds. Serves 4-6.

Four Cheese Crostini
Crostini Quattro Formaggi

Ingredients

½ lb. Parmigiano Reggiano, grated
½ lb. Asiago cheese, grated
½ lb. Pecorino Romano cheese, grated
½ lb. Mascarpone cheese
⅓ cup extra virgin olive oil
fresh ground pepper to taste
box of toasted crostini
      (or make your own from a long baguette)

Instructions

Place all cheeses in a food processor and add the olive oil. Process on high for 2 minutes until well mixed. Remove from work bowl and transfer to a serving bowl. Add fresh pepper to taste. Spread onto toasted crostini or your favorite crackers, and serve with cold glasses of Prosecco. Serves 4-6.

Crostini with Fig Spread, Caramelized Onions and Gorgonzola

Crostini con Crema di Fiche Cipolla e Gorgonzola

Ingredients

2 Tbsp. butter
2 Tbsp. regular olive oil
1 large Vidalia onion cut into thin slices
1 Tbsp. dark brown sugar

1 jar fig spread with walnuts
6-8 oz. crumbled gorgonzola cheese
   (or blue cheese, for a milder flavor)
1 long seedless French bread

Instructions

Melt butter with the oil in a large frying pan over medium heat. When hot, add sliced onion and stir to coat. Cook over medium-high heat for ten minutes. Add brown sugar and stir well until melted and all onions are coated. Lower heat to low-medium and slow cook onions, stirring often, for 30-35 minutes. Onions will greatly shrink in size; they will be moist and caramelized.

Preheat oven to 350° halfway through onion cooking time. Diagonally slice French bread into ¼-inch slices. Coat two cookie sheets with an olive oil-based cooking spray. Arrange slices among the two sheets. Lightly spray toasts. Bake in 350° oven for five minutes.

Remove from oven and cool slightly. Using a butter knife, carefully spread about 1 Tbsp. fig spread on bottom side of crostini, which will be somewhat crispier than the top. When put back into the oven, the top side will crisp. *Note*: Fig spread is very thick. When spreading on toasts, be careful not to break them in half.

When onions are cooked, spoon 1 tsp. onions on each fig-covered crostini. Put a teaspoonful of cheese over onions and bake until cheese is melted, about 10 minutes. Serve warm. Makes 2 dozen.

Artichoke Heart Spread

Carciofini tapenade

This spread is also excellent over pasta.

Ingredients

2 14-oz. cans artichoke hearts
½ lb. Mascarpone cheese
12 basil leaves
6 cloves garlic, peeled
½ cup extra virgin olive oil
salt and pepper to taste

Instructions

Drain artichoke hearts, squeezing out any excess liquid. Place artichokes in food processor, then add the Mascarpone cheese, basil, garlic, extra virgin olive oil, salt and pepper. Process for 2-3 minutes on high until well combined. Transfer to a bowl and serve with crostini or fresh vegetables. Serves 4-6.

Baked Clams with Bacon
Vongole Ripiene

Decorative clam shells used for baking can be found in houseware stores, or you can ask your local fishmonger for shells (be sure to clean them thoroughly).

Ingredients

2 cans minced clams (drain liquid and save)
½ cup seasoned bread crumbs
¼ cup grated Parmigiano, plus extra for sprinkling
1 medium onion, chopped
½ green pepper, ½ red pepper and ½ yellow pepper, chopped
1 garlic clove, minced
8 slices bacon
salt and pepper to taste

Instructions

Preheat oven to 350°. Fry bacon in skillet. When crisp, remove from pan and let cool. Add chopped onion, peppers and garlic to 2-3 Tbsp. remaining bacon fat. Cook until soft. Add clams, cheese, salt and pepper. Cook two minutes. Pour in clam broth. When mixture starts to bubble, add bread crumbs and stir constantly until thoroughly mixed.

Fill clam shells. Sprinkle a little more grating cheese on top. Crumble cooled bacon. Sprinkle each clam shell with the bacon. Bake 20 minutes. Makes about one dozen, depending on size of clam shell.

Basic Stuffed Mushrooms
Funghi Imbottiti

Ingredients

2 dozen large white mushrooms, stems removed
1 cup seasoned bread crumbs
½ cup grated Parmigiano, and more for sprinkling
1 Tbsp. garlic powder
fresh ground pepper to taste
1 stick softened butter
paprika

Instructions

Preheat oven to 400°. In each mushroom cavity, place a small amount of softened butter. In a small mixing bowl, combine bread crumbs, cheese, garlic powder and pepper. With a small spoon, fill the center of each mushroom with filling mixture, pressing down with thumb. When each mushroom is filled, sprinkle with a little more parmigiano, sprinkle with a little paprika, and place a small piece of butter on top. Bake for 30 minutes.

Fried Shiitake Mushrooms
Funghi Fritti

These mushrooms are delicious dipped in marinara or fra diavola sauce and served as an antipasti. Also excellent as a side dish to steak, or in a sandwich on crusty bread with fresh mozzarella, tomatoes, olive oil and basil.

Ingredients

12 extra large shiitake mushrooms,
    stems removed, mushrooms left whole or cut in half
3 eggs
1 Tbsp. flour
½ cup heavy cream
1 lb. homestyle seasoned breadcrumbs
1 Tbsp. chopped fresh Italian parsley
fresh ground pepper to taste
2 Tbsp. Pecorino Romano cheese, grated
canola oil for frying
salt and fresh ground pepper to taste

Instructions

Beat the eggs in a shallow bowl, and then add the flour, heavy cream, chopped parsley, Pecorino Romano cheese, and salt and pepper. Mix well. Dip each mushroom into the egg mixture, and then press into the seasoned breadcrumbs to coat. Set aside.

Pour about 1 inch of canola oil into a 12-inch nonstick frying pan, and heat until a sprinkling of breadcrumbs fry quickly. Add the mushrooms in batches, frying 3 to 4 at a time for about two minutes on each side.

Instead of pan frying, you can lightly spray the mushrooms with olive oil and bake in a 350° oven for 30 minutes until crisp.

Serves 4-6.

Grilled Portabella Mushrooms with Fresh Spinach, Red Onion, Garlic and Goat Cheese

Funghi Arrostiti con Spinaci Cipolla Aglio e Formaggio di Capra

Ingredients

4 portabella mushrooms
1 cup olive oil plus 3 Tbsp. extra
1 medium sized red onion, thinly sliced
6 cloves garlic, chopped
1½ slivered sun-dried tomatoes

4 thick slices soft goat cheese
3-4 bunches fresh spinach
4 Tbsp. chopped fresh Italian parsley
Salt and fresh ground pepper to taste

Instructions

Remove stems from portabellas. Marinate in a ziplock bag with one cup olive oil and the garlic for a half hour at room temperature. If sun-dried tomatoes are hard, soften them in a cup of very hot water until they are pliable and soft. Thoroughly wash and dry spinach, and remove tough stems.

In a large skillet, heat 3 Tbsp. olive oil on medium heat. When hot, add sliced onion and cook 5 minutes, stirring. Remove the mushrooms from the bag and set aside. Add the discarded garlic from the oil to the onions in the skillet, then add the drained sun-dried tomatoes and stir. Add the spinach and cook 5-7 minutes more until spinach is wilted.

While spinach cooks, heat grill or indoor grill pan to medium high heat. Grill portabellas topside down for 7-10 minutes, depending on size and thickness. Turn over and grill another 10 minutes or until tender. Place one slice goat cheese on center of mushroom.

Close lid on grill, or if cooking indoors, transfer grill pan to a preheated 350° oven. Cook mushrooms 5-7 minutes until cheese is very soft and slightly melted. Place a generous portion of onion mixture on each of four plates, covering the bottom. Place a mushroom on the center of each. Sprinkle with fresh parsley, salt and pepper. Serves 4.

White Bean and Sun-dried Tomato Dip with Pita

Pure di Cannellini e Pomodori Secchi

Ingredients

2 Tbsp. regular olive oil
1 small onion, chopped
1 clove minced garlic
1 15.5-oz. can cannellini beans, drained and rinsed
¼ tsp. crushed red pepper flakes
1 Tbsp. finely chopped fresh rosemary
1 cup oil-packed sun-dried tomatoes coarsely chopped
¼ tsp. salt

fresh ground pepper to taste
1 cup hot water
½ cup extra virgin olive oil
Juice of ½ lemon
fresh chopped parsley
toasted pitas or store bought pita chips
fresh vegetables for dipping if desired

Instructions

Cook onions in 2 Tbsp. olive oil until softened. Add minced garlic, stirring 30 seconds. Add beans and red pepper flakes. Stir. Cook with the onion and garlic 3-5 minutes. Remove from heat and let cool slightly.

Put bean mixture, rosemary and sun-dried tomatoes into a blender or food processor. Add salt and pepper, lemon juice, hot water and extra virgin olive oil. Blend until ingredients are mixed and dip is thickened and smooth. If the mixture is too thick, add more hot water and blend. Transfer dip to a serving bowl and garnish with fresh chopped parsley. Serve with toasted pita chips and fresh vegetables. Yields approximately 4 cups.

Joe's Summer Salsa

Insalata di Stagione alla Giuseppe

Kerriann's Note: Although this is not an Italian recipe, I've included it because I make it every August for Joe Baldanza, who loves spicy hot dishes! It's best when tomatoes are at their ripest. I grow my own tomatoes, and a variety of hot peppers — but if you have no garden, just visit one of the many farm stands that sell wonderful produce. It really makes a difference in this recipe.

Caution: Please wear rubber gloves when cutting the hot peppers and dealing with cutting boards, knives, etc. Habañeros are extremely hot, but give an exceptional and very different taste to this salsa.

Ingredients

3 large ripened tomatoes, chopped
½ green pepper, chopped
½ red pepper, chopped
½ yellow pepper, chopped
2-3 jalapeño peppers, finely chopped
1-2 long red or green chili peppers, finely chopped
1-2 habañero peppers (depending on how hot you want your salsa), minced

2 cooked and cooled fresh corn on the cob, kernels removed
½ large onion, chopped
1 small can tomato sauce
6 drops Tabasco or other hot sauce
½ cup chopped cilantro

Instructions

Combine all ingredients, mixing thoroughly. Serve at room temperature with tortilla chips. Yield: approximately 6 cups. Can be stored in refrigerator for several days.

SOUPS AND STEWS

Zuppe e Stufati

Italian White Bean Soup

Zuppa di Cannellini alla Italiana

Ingredients

1 Tbsp. olive oil
1 medium sized onion, finely chopped
1 celery stalk, finely chopped
1 clove minced garlic
2 15.5 oz. cans cannellini beans, drained and rinsed
2 14 oz. cans chicken broth
fresh ground pepper
⅛ tsp. dried thyme leaves

1 bunch fresh spinach
1 Tbsp. fresh lemon juice
freshly grated Parmigiano cheese

Instructions

In a large saucepan, heat oil over medium heat. Add onion and celery and cook 5-8 minutes until tender, stirring occasionally. Add garlic and stir 30 seconds. Add beans, chicken broth, pepper, thyme and 2 cups water. Heat to boiling over high heat. Reduce heat to low and simmer uncovered for 15 minutes.

Using a slotted spoon, remove two cups of bean-vegetable mixture from soup and set aside. In a blender, blend the remaining soup in small batches at low speed until smooth, pouring soup into a large bowl after each batch. Return soup to saucepan, stir in reserved beans and vegetables. Heat to boiling over high heat, stirring occasionally. Stir in spinach and cook 1 minute or until spinach is wilted. Stir in lemon juice and remove from heat. Serve with Parmigiano cheese. Serves 4.

To make a heartier soup, add ¾ cup tubetti pasta to soup at the end and cook until al dente.

Escarole Soup with Cannellini Beans
Zuppa di Fagioli

Ingredients

½ cup extra virgin olive oil
2 medium white onions, chopped
2 Tbsp. chopped garlic
3 15 oz. cans cannellini beans, undrained
2 bunches fresh escarole, chopped
2 cubes vegetable bouillon
5 cups vegetable broth
1 28 oz. can tomato puree
salt and pepper to taste
toasted garlic bread, optional

Instructions

In a small stockpot, bring water to a boil. Wash escarole, then remove bottom stems and coarsely chop. Cook escarole for about 15 minutes until tender, and drain.

In an 8-quart stockpot, heat olive oil over medium heat. Add onions and garlic, and sauté until soft. Add the tomato puree, vegetable stock and vegetable bouillon. Stir. Add the salt and pepper. Bring to a boil. Reduce heat and add the undrained beans. Add the chopped escarole and cook 25-30 minutes.

Soup can be served with a slice of toasted garlic bread placed in the center of each soup bowl. Serves 4-6.

Lentil Spinach Soup
Zuppa di Lenticchie con Spinaci

This soup is a hearty meal on its own, or serve with bread and a salad.

Ingredients

¼ cup extra virgin olive oil
4 large cloves garlic, chopped fine
1 large white onion, chopped
2 large carrots, peeled and chopped
1 28 oz. can crushed tomatoes
6 cups vegetable broth
1 lb. bag dry lentils, rinsed
6 cups fresh baby spinach
Salt and pepper to taste

Instructions

In a 6-quart stockpot, heat olive oil over medium heat. Add onions and garlic and sauté 2-3 minutes over medium low heat. Add carrots and cook for another 2-3 minutes. Add crushed tomatoes, vegetable broth and lentils and bring to a boil. Reduce heat and simmer, covered, for 25 minutes or until lentils are tender. Stir. Add salt and pepper to taste.

Add the fresh spinach and cook until wilted, about 3 minutes. Serves 4-6.

Gazpacho with Homemade Croutons
Zuppa di Gazpacho

Ingredients

1 large can tomato juice
2 beef bouillon cubes
1 tomato, chopped
1 small cucumber, unpared, chopped
1 green bell pepper, chopped
1 small onion, chopped
4 Tbsp. wine vinegar
2 Tbsp. vegetable oil
1 tsp. salt

1 Tbsp. Worcestershire sauce
6 drops Tabasco sauce
For croutons:
1 loaf Italian bread
½ cup olive oil
4 tsps. dried oregano or Italian seasonings
1 tsp. each, garlic powder and onion powder
2 Tbsp. grated Parmigiano
½ tsp. each, salt and pepper

Instructions

Note: This healthy, cold soup should be made a day ahead. In a large pot, heat tomato juice and bouillon cubes until boiling and cubes are dissolved. Stir in wine vinegar, vegetable oil, salt, Worcestershire sauce and Tabasco. Add vegetables to blender or food processor, adding tomato juice for liquid. Blend all together. Stir and put in large bowl. Chill overnight. Serve the next day with croutons. Serves 6-8 depending on portion size.

For croutons, preheat oven to 350°. Pour olive oil in a 1-gallon ziplock bag. Put all dry ingredients in a second 1 gallon ziplock bag and shake until well combined. Cube day-old Italian bread into bite-sized pieces. Put cubes in bag with olive oil. Shake vigorously until all the oil is absorbed and bread pieces are thoroughly coated. Transfer bread cubes to second bag containing dry ingredients. Shake vigorously until well coated. Place croutons in a single layer on a cookie sheet and bake for 20 minutes, turning croutons twice to bake evenly. Cool croutons completely. Store in an air-tight container. They will keep for several weeks at room temperature.

Neapolitan Seafood Stew

Frutta di Mare alla Napoletana

Ingredients

4 coarsely chopped garlic cloves
3 minced garlic cloves for toasts
2 Tbsp. olive oil, plus ¼ cup for toasts
1 ½ cups chopped onion
1 yellow bell pepper, coarsely chopped
2 tsp. dried oregano
¼ tsp. crushed red pepper flakes
1 cup dry red wine
1 28-oz. can crushed plum tomatoes

6 slices Italian bread
2 8-oz. bottles clam juice
⅓ cup Italian parsley, chopped,
    plus more for garnish
2 dozen uncooked, cleaned shrimp
1 ½ dozen Little Neck clams
2 dozen mussels
½ pound bay scallops
salt and pepper to taste

Instructions

Preheat oven to 350°. Heat 2 Tbsp. olive oil in a large pot on medium heat. When hot, add onion, bell pepper, garlic, oregano and red pepper flakes. Cook 5-8 minutes until soft, stirring occasionally. Add the wine and increase heat to medium high. Cook 5 minutes until the wine is reduced by about half. Add the tomatoes, water, clam juice and salt and pepper to taste. Bring to a boil. Reduce heat to low medium. Add shrimp, clams and mussels. Cook about 3 minutes until shrimp are pink and clams and mussels are beginning to open. Add the bay scallops and parsley and cook another 3-5 minutes.

While the stew is cooking, make the garlic toast. Spray a cookie sheet with an olive oil based cooking spray. Place Italian bread slices on cookie sheet. Combine ¼ cup of olive oil and 3 cloves minced garlic in small bowl. Using a pastry brush or spoon, spread olive oil mixture over each bread slice. Bake in oven for 10 minutes, and then broil on low for 30 seconds to one minute, watching carefully so toasts don't burn. Place a toast in the bottom of each soup bowl. Ladle soup over bread and garnish with fresh chopped parsley. Serves 4.

Pasta and Chick Pea Soup

Zuppa di Ceci con Pasta

Ingredients

½ cup extra virgin olive oil, plus extra
4 large garlic cloves, sliced
1 medium white onion, chopped
1 Tbsp. chopped fresh rosemary
crushed red pepper to taste
2 Tbsp. Arborio rice flour (see below)
1 Tbsp. tomato paste

2½ cups vegetable broth
2 15-oz. cans chick peas, undrained
1 lb. mezzi rigatoni pasta
salt and pepper to taste
¼ cup fresh Italian parsley, chopped
shaved Parmigiano Reggiano

Instructions

In a mini chop or processor, grind approximately 4 Tbsp. of Arborio rice until you have 2 Tbsp. of *Arborio rice flour*. In a 6-quart pot, heat ½ cup olive oil over medium heat. Add the garlic, onions, rosemary and crushed red pepper. Sauté until garlic and onions are tender, about 2-3 minutes. Add Arborio rice flour and mix well. Add tomato paste and vegetable broth to the pot. Stir. Bring to a boil, and add undrained chick peas. Bring back to a low boil and add the pasta. Cook until pasta is al dente. Add salt and pepper to taste. Ladle into bowls, and garnish with fresh parsley and a drizzle of extra virgin olive oil. Serve with freshly shaved Parmigiano Reggiano. Serves 4-6.

Bean and Pasta Soup
Pasta Fagioli

Ingredients

4 Tbsp. extra virgin olive oil
4 large garlic cloves, sliced
1 medium red onion, chopped
2 stalks celery, diced
2 Tbsp. Arborio rice flour (see below)
crushed red pepper to taste

1 28-oz. can tomato puree
4 cups vegetable broth
2 15-oz. cans cannellini beans, unrinsed
1 lb. ditalini pasta
fresh Italian parsley, chopped, for garnish
salt and pepper to taste

Instructions

In a mini chop or processor, grind approximately 4 Tbsp. Arborio rice until you have 2 Tbsp. of *Arborio rice flour.* In a 6-quart pot, heat olive oil over medium heat, then add garlic, onions, celery, and crushed red pepper. Cook until tender, about 2-3 minutes.

Add Arborio rice flour, and mix. Add tomato puree, and 4 cups vegetable broth. Bring to a boil, and add the unrinsed beans. Bring back to a low boil and add the ditalini pasta. Cook until tender. Add salt and pepper to taste.

Ladle into bowls and garnish with fresh parsley and a drizzle of extra virgin olive oil. Serve with fresh shaved Parmigiano Reggiano. Serves 4-6.

Roasted Tomato, Onion and Vegetable Soup with Goat Cheese Dumplings

Zuppa con Pomodoro e Vegetali Arrostiti

Ingredients

2 carrots cut in half lengthwise
3 medium sized onions, halved
2 lbs. plum tomatoes
4 garlic cloves
3 4-oz. logs soft goat cheese
¼ cup fresh bread crumbs

1 large egg, beaten
3 cups chicken broth
1 Tbsp. fresh chives, finely chopped
1 Tbsp. fresh Italian parsley, finely chopped
1 Tbsp. fresh basil, finely chopped
salt and pepper to taste

Instructions

Preheat oven to 400°. On a large cookie sheet sprayed with an olive oil based cooking spray, place the carrots and onions, cut side down. Add the garlic cloves to the pan. Slice off a small piece of the top of each tomato, then stand flat side down on pan with other vegetables. Roast in oven for 1 hour.

For the dumplings, mash goat cheese in a bowl with a fork. Mix in the breadcrumbs and fresh herbs. Season with salt and pepper. Mix in the beaten egg. Taking a teaspoonful at a time, mold the goat cheese into small dumplings and set aside. When the vegetables are cooked, cool them slightly and put them in a blender. Add the chicken broth. Blend until thoroughly mixed. Over a sieve, strain vegetable mixture over a saucepan. Heat the soup until simmering. Season with salt and pepper. Add the dumplings and poach them until firm, 3-4 minutes. Carefully ladle into soup bowls and serve immediately. Serves 4-6.

Roasted Vegetable Soup

Zuppa con vegetale arrostito

This healthy soup is a delicious way to eat more vegetables.

Ingredients

2 yellow squash, diced into ½ inch pieces
2 green zucchini, diced into ½ inch pieces
2 red peppers, diced into ½ inch pieces
4 large peeled carrots, diced into ½ inch pieces
1 large onion, chopped
2 bunches asparagus cut into ½ inch rounds
2 large potatoes, diced into ½ inch pieces
4 large cloves garlic, chopped

1 28-oz. can crushed tomatoes
8 cups vegetable broth
1 cup extra virgin olive oil
salt and pepper to taste

Instructions

Preheat oven to 375°. Toss all the diced vegetables, including the garlic, in a large bowl with the cup of olive oil. On two baking sheets, spread the vegetables in a single layer and add salt and pepper to taste. Bake for 25-30 minutes until vegetables are tender.

Remove vegetables from the oven and place in a 6-quart stockpot. Add the crushed tomatoes and vegetable broth. Bring to a boil, and then lower to a simmer and cook for 25 minutes. Add salt and pepper if desired. Ladle into bowls. Serves 4-6.

Wild Mushroom Soup in Puff Pastry
Zuppa con Funghi di Bosco

A variation of a simple yet terrific soup; adding the puff pastry makes it an elegant presentation.

Ingredients

2 Tbsp. butter
1 small onion, finely chopped
1 garlic clove, minced
1 lb. mixed mushrooms, sliced – white, cremini, shiitake
5 cups chicken broth
⅔ cup good quality sherry
2 Tbsp. chopped fresh thyme, plus extra for garnish
salt and fresh ground pepper to taste
1 box frozen puff pastry sheets, defrosted

Instructions

Melt the butter in a large saucepan. Add the onion and garlic and cook, stirring occasionally for about 3 minutes until onion is soft, but not browned. Add the sliced mushrooms and cook stirring occasionally for 3-5 minutes. Add the broth, sherry, thyme and salt and pepper. Bring to a boil, then cover and simmer gently for 10 minutes. Preheat oven to 400°.

Pour soup into 4 ovenproof crocks, to about ½ inch from the top, so puff pastry will not sink into soup. Cut 4 equal squares of puff pastry large enough to cover entire top of crock, with some extra to fold over the sides. Carefully place each square over soup, pulling tightly over crock, folding pastry slightly over sides.

Put crocks on a cookie sheet and bake for about 15 minutes until pastry is golden and puffed. Serve immediately, putting crocks on heat-tolerant plates. Serves 4.

SALADS

Insalate

Arugula Salad
Insalata di Arugula

This can serve as a main course with bread or breadsticks, or as a first course.

Ingredients

3-4 bunches fresh arugula
15 thin slices imported prosciutto
chunk of Parmigiano cheese
fresh juice from ½ lemon
extra virgin olive oil

Instructions

Thoroughly wash and dry arugula leaves. Tear into bite sized pieces and lay on a platter. Arrange prosciutto slices around the arugula, making an appetizing presentation. Using a potato peeler, thinly slice 1-2 inch curls of parmigiano, making as many as you like. Arrange over arugula and prosciutto. Drizzle the lemon juice over salad. Carefully pour extra virgin olive oil in a slow, thin stream over salad until leaves are moist but not soaking. Serves two as a main course, and four as a first course.

Chick Pea Salad
Insalata di Ceci

A wonderful summer side dish, or add to a green salad for a delicious twist.

Ingredients

3 15 oz. cans chick peas
2 stalks celery, chopped
1 large red onion, chopped
4 cloves garlic, chopped extra fine
1 Tbsp. grated lemon zest
¼ cup freshly squeezed lemon juice
2 Tbsp. chopped fresh Italian parsley
4 Tbsp. extra virgin olive oil
Salt and pepper to taste

Instructions

Rinse chick peas and drain well, then place in a large bowl. Add remaining ingredients and mix well. Refrigerate until chilled. Serves 4-6.

Endive Salad with Walnuts and Gorgonzola
Insalata di Indivia con Noci e Gorgonzola

Ingredients

6 endives cut into julienne strips
½ cup walnut oil
¼ white wine vinegar
juice of one fresh lemon
1 Tbsp. Dijon mustard
1 cup gorgonzola cheese, crumbled
1 cup Granny Smith apple, cubed
½ cup walnuts, toasted
½ cup fresh Italian parsley, chopped

Instructions

Preheat oven to 350°. Toast walnuts on a cookie sheet 5-8 minutes until fragrant. (Toasting the nuts brings out their flavor). Let cool.

Whisk together the oil, vinegar, lemon juice and mustard in a small bowl. In a large salad bowl, pour the dressing over the julienne endives and gently toss to coat. Place salad on four or six salad plates. Sprinkle each salad with the cheese, apple cubes, walnuts and parsley. Serves 4-6.

Grandpa D'Amato's Caesar Salad with Homemade Croutons

Insalata di Cesare del Nonno

This traditional Caesar salad recipe was passed down from Kerriann's grandfather; she added the homemade croutons. Sliced grilled chicken breasts can also be added, for a heartier meal.

Ingredients

8 large romaine lettuce leaves
1 small clove garlic, minced
¼ tsp. anchovy paste
1 egg yolk
juice of ½ lemon
¼ cup olive oil
grated Parmigiano
fresh ground pepper
homemade croutons (see p. 19)

Instructions

Mince garlic and rub in a large salad bowl. Add anchovy paste and whisk. Add egg yolk and lemon juice and whisk again. Add olive oil and whisk again. Tear romaine lettuce leaves into bite sized pieces and add to dressing. Toss well and add a generous amount of Parmigiano to coat. Sprinkle with croutons and freshly ground pepper. Makes four appetizer portions or two main dishes.

Farfalle with Sun-Dried Tomatoes and Smoked Mozzarella

Farfalle con Pomodori Secchi e Mozzarella Affumicata

A great summer side salad.

Ingredients

1 lb. smoked mozzarella cut into ½- inch cubes
2 bunches broccoli rabe
½ cup extra virgin olive oil
4 cloves garlic, chopped
1 medium red onion, chopped
½ lb. sun-dried tomatoes, chopped
1 ½ lbs. farfalle pasta (bowtie shaped)
1 cup fresh basil, chopped
salt and pepper to taste

Instructions

Bring a 6-quart stockpot of water to a boil. Add pasta and cook until al dente. Drain the pasta and rinse with cold water to cool. Set aside in a shallow salad bowl.

In a medium frying pan, heat olive oil over medium heat and add garlic, onions and sun-dried tomatoes. Sauté 4-5 minutes. Remove from heat and set aside to cool. Add the sautéed mixture and smoked mozzarella to the pasta. Add fresh basil, salt and pepper to taste. Toss. Serves 4-6.

Grape Tomato Salad with Capers
Insalata di Pomodori con Chiapperi

A light side dish to accompany a barbecue. Wonderful in the summer when tomatoes are in season.

Ingredients

3 lbs. grape tomatoes, cut in half
3 stalks celery, chopped
1 large red onion, chopped
4 cloves garlic, chopped
2 Tbsp. capers
½ lb. shredded Romano cheese
1 tsp. dried oregano
½ cup chopped basil
½ cup extra virgin olive oil
salt and pepper to taste

Instructions

In a medium-sized shallow bowl, combine all ingredients, reserving ⅓ cup Romano cheese. Toss thoroughly, and let stand for 20 minutes at room temperature. Add remaining Romano cheese to the top before serving. Serves 4-6.

Grilled Portabella Salad
Insalata di Funghi alla Griglia

Ingredients

½ cup olive oil
2 cloves garlic, minced
¼ cup extra virgin olive oil for dressing
2 Tbsp. raspberry vinaigrette
¼ tsp. brown sugar, packed
salt and fresh ground pepper to taste
6 medium sized portabella mushrooms, stems removed
5 cups mesclun greens
1 Tbsp. grated lemon zest

Instructions

Preheat a grill or indoor grill pan to medium high heat. Marinate mushrooms in ½ cup olive oil and minced garlic for 20-30 minutes at room temperature.

To make the dressing, blend ¼ cup extra virgin olive oil, raspberry vinaigrette, 1 Tbsp. water, brown sugar, salt and pepper.

When grill or grill pan is hot, grill mushrooms on medium heat 7-10 minutes per side, depending on size and thickness of mushrooms. When cooked, transfer to a cutting board and slice mushrooms diagonally, about ¼ inch thick.

Toss the mesclun greens with the dressing and arrange on 4 salad plates. Arrange the mushroom slices on the greens. Season with salt and pepper and grated lemon zest. Serves 4.

Italian Chopped Salad
Insalata alla Italiano

Ingredients

5 plum tomatoes, diced
2 Belgian endives, chopped
12 plain mozzarella bocconcini, cut in half
2 cups arugula, chopped
1 cup radicchio, chopped
1 cup roasted red peppers, chopped

For vinaigrette:
2 Tbsp. Sherry wine vinegar
1 Tbsp. minced shallots
1 Tbsp. Dijon mustard
¼ cup extra virgin olive oil
salt and fresh ground pepper to taste

Instructions

In a large bowl, combine all salad ingredients. For the vinaigrette, whisk vinegar, shallots and mustard in a small bowl. Gradually whisk in olive oil. Season with salt and fresh ground pepper. Toss salad with enough vinaigrette to coat.

Serves 4 as a first course, or 2 as a main course.

Orzo Salad with Fresh Dill and Chick Peas

Insalata di orzo con dill e ceci

This delicious and easy to make summer salad can be served as a side dish or entrée.

Ingredients

1 lb. orzo pasta
2 15-oz. cans chick peas
½ cup extra virgin olive oil
½ cup fresh chopped dill
2 Tbsp. lemon zest
¼ cup fresh lemon juice
2 Tbsp. fresh chopped Italian parsley
1 chopped red onion
salt and pepper to taste

Instructions

Bring 3 quarts of water to a boil. Boil orzo pasta for about 8-10 minutes until cooked. Drain and run cold water over pasta until it is cooled. Strain and place in a large bowl.

Drain and rinse chick peas and put in the bowl with the orzo. Add extra virgin olive oil, dill, lemon zest, lemon juice, chopped parsley, onion, salt and pepper. Mix well. Serve chilled or at room temperature. Serves 4-6.

Sal's Seafood Salad

Frutta di Mare alla Sal

A traditional Italian favorite, best made one day ahead to allow flavors to blend in the refrigerator.

Ingredients

½ yellow pepper, chopped
½ red pepper, chopped
3 stalks of celery, chopped
1 large red onion, chopped
6 cloves of garlic, sliced
1 Tbsp. grated lemon zest
juice of 3 fresh lemons
½ cup chopped fresh Italian parsley

½ lb. pitted calamata olives, sliced in half
1 cup extra virgin olive oil
2 lbs. fresh calamari rings
1 ½ lb. cleaned shrimp
1 lb. mussels
1 28-oz. can of sliced scungilli (conch), rinsed
salt and pepper to taste

Instructions

In a large shallow bowl, combine all ingredients from the peppers through the olive oil. Set aside.

Steam the mussels in a covered shallow pan of water until opened. Let the mussels cool and remove meat. Rinse in cool water to remove any sand.

Fill a 6-quart stockpot halfway with water. Add a pinch of salt. Cover and bring to a boil. Add calamari and boil for 10-15 minutes until tender. Add the shrimp and cook for 2 minutes more. Remove from heat, drain and place in cold water. Let cool and drain again. Add the seafood to the bowl with the vegetables, and add the rinsed scungilli. Stir to combine. Serves 4-6.

PIZZA, BREADS, AND PANINIS

Pizza, Pane e Panini

Grilled Mortadella Panini with Fresh Mozzarella, Tomato and Basil

Panini alla Griglia con Mortadella, Mozzarella, Pomodoro, e Basilico

This makes a wonderful lunch or dinner. It's also excellent for a boat trip or picnic. You don't need a panini grill to make this.

Ingredients

2 long French baguettes
½ lb. black olive spread
18 thin slices of Mortadella
20 ¼-inch thick slices of fresh mozzarella
20 very thin slices of beefsteak tomato
1 red onion sliced very thin
20 leaves fresh basil
extra virgin olive oil
dried oregano and fresh ground pepper to taste

Instructions

Preheat oven to 350°. Heat a cast iron grill pan over medium heat. Place 1 slice of mortadella in the pan at a time and grill for 30 seconds on each side. Finish all slices and set aside. Slice bread lengthwise and toast open-faced in a 350° oven for 5 minutes. Remove from oven and apply olive spread on each of the cut sides.

Begin to layer sandwich ingredients on one side of each of the baguettes: start with the mortadella, then the mozzarella, tomato slices, onions, fresh basil, and lastly the oregano and black pepper to taste. Lightly drizzle olive oil over the ingredients.

Close the sandwich and cut each loaf into 4 or 5 sections. Serves 4-6.

Foccacia with Caramelized Onions, Prosciutto and Asiago Cheese

Foccacia con cipolla, prosciutto, e formaggio asiago

A savory start to almost any meal. Experiment by varying the cheese type.

Ingredients

2 lbs. pizza dough at room temperature
¼ stick butter
2 Tbsp. olive oil
3 cloves garlic, chopped
2 large onions, sliced thin
6 thin slices Prosciutto di Parma, cut into strips
fresh ground pepper to taste
½ lb. shredded Asiago cheese

Instructions

Preheat oven to 375°. Stretch pizza dough across a cookie sheet brushed with olive oil. Set in a warm place. In a non-stick frying pan, heat the olive oil and butter over medium heat. When butter is melted and oil is hot, add the garlic and onions. Add the prosciutto and cook an additional 3 minutes. Re-stretch dough on cookie sheet, if necessary, and bake for 10 minutes. Remove from the oven and spread onions and prosciutto mixture over the dough. Place back in the oven and bake for an additional 20-25 minutes. Before serving, sprinkle Asiago cheese and fresh ground pepper over foccacia. Slice with a pizza cutter and enjoy! Serves 4-6.

Grilled Panini with Fig Spread, Shaved Parmigiano Reggiano and Aged Balsamic Vinegar

Panini alla Griglia con Crema di Fiche, Parmigiano Reggiano, e Aceto Balsamico

The combination of the sweet fig spread, the aged balsamic vinegar and the sharp Parmigiano Reggiano creates a complex flavor. These sandwiches are addictive!

Ingredients

2 long French baguettes
1 jar fig spread
½ lb. shaved Parmigiano Reggiano
12 thin slices of Prosciutto Parma
Aged balsamic vinegar
2 bunches or 1 bag baby arugula

Cooking Instructions

Preheat a panini grill to 375°. Slice bread lengthwise. Apply fig spread to both cut sides of bread. Begin to layer the sandwich ingredients on the bread, starting with the prosciutto, then the shaved Parmigiano, and then the arugula. Lightly drizzle aged balsamic vinegar over the ingredients.

Cut sandwiches into sections that will fit into the panini grill. Place the sandwiches in the grill, close lid, and press down. Cook until bread is toasted and ingredients are warm. Repeat until all the sandwiches have been toasted.

Cut each sandwich into 4 sections and serve. Serves 4-6.

Grilled Panini with Sun-dried Tomatoes and Smoked Mozzarella

Panini alla griglia con pomodori secchi e mozzarella affumicata

Ingredients

2 Italian hero rolls
⅓ lb. smoked mozzarella
½ lb. sun-dried tomatoes
¼ lb. sun-dried tomato spread
½ red onion thinly sliced
6 pre-grilled portabella mushrooms
fresh baby arugula
olive oil for drizzling

Instructions

Preheat panini grill to 375°. Slice hero rolls lengthwise and pre-toast on the grill for 2 minutes, face down. Drizzle olive oil on open sides of the rolls. Spread both sides with the sun-dried tomato spread, then layer portabella mushrooms, sun-dried tomatoes, arugula, red onions and smoked mozzarella on open sides of each roll. Close the sandwich and place back on the hot grill. Keep grill closed for several minutes until ingredients are warm. Serves 2.

Grilled Panini alla Italiana
Panini alla Griglia alla Italiana

A light dinner or delicious lunch. Serve with a side of pasta or a green salad.

Ingredients

2 Italian hero rolls
⅓ lb. hot capicollo, sliced thin
⅓ lb. Mortadella, sliced thin
⅓ lb. imported sopressata, sliced thin
⅓ lb. ham capicollo, sliced thin
⅓ lb. sliced imported provolone
½ lb. marinated roasted red peppers
olive oil for drizzling
balsamic vinegar for drizzling

Instructions

Preheat panini grill to 375°. Slice rolls lengthwise and pre-toast on the pannini grill for 2 minutes, face down. Drizzle olive oil and balsamic vinegar on both cut sides of the bread. Place roasted red peppers on one side of each hero roll. Then layer all the cold cuts on top of the peppers, placing the cheese on top.

Close the sandwiches and place them back on the hot grill. Close the grill and cook for several minutes until ingredients are warm. Serves 2.

Onion-Rosemary Flatbread
Focaccia Schiacciata con Cipolla e Rosmarino

This is always a hit with company.

Ingredients

1 pizza dough
¼ cup fresh rosemary (do not substitute dried)
1 medium Vidalia onion, chopped
extra virgin olive oil
Kosher salt
fresh ground pepper to taste

Instructions

Set pizza dough at room temperature for at least an hour until dough is supple. Preheat oven to 400°. Lightly oil a cookie sheet with olive oil. Work pizza dough into a free-form rectangular shape and place on cookie sheet.

Chop onion, then sprinkle over entire dough. Chop fresh rosemary leaves and sprinkle over onions. Sprinkle kosher salt and fresh ground pepper over dough. Pour a slow, thin stream of extra virgin olive oil all across the top. Bake for 15-20 minutes until golden brown. Cut into large squares and serve warm.

Pan-Fried Pizza Margherita
Pizza in padella Margherita

Delicious as an appetizer, or as a main dish. A children's favorite too.

Ingredients

1 tsp. olive oil
1 lb. pizza dough, room temperature
1 pint marinara sauce
½ lb. thinly sliced fresh mozzarella (1 day old, chilled)
¼ cup Pecorino Romano cheese, grated
fresh basil, cut into strips or chopped

Instructions

Put 1 tsp. olive oil in a 12-inch non-stick fry pan. Stretch out the dough to the diameter of the pan. Place dough in the pan and reshape and flatten to fit pan. Cook both sides for 3-4 minutes over low-medium heat until dough is cooked through and it is crispy on both sides. Thinly spread marinara over the dough, then sprinkle with Pecorino cheese. Lay mozzarella slices on top, then sprinkle with the basil. Cook on low heat until cheese is melted, or remove from the non-stick pan and bake in a 350° oven for 5-6 minutes. Serves 2 as a main course or 4-6 as an appetizer.

Pizza with Goat Cheese, Mozzarella, Parmigiano and Gorgonzola

Pizza Quattro Formaggi

Ingredients

1 pizza dough
½ cup soft goat cheese
½ cup shredded fresh mozzarella
½ cup crumbled gorgonzola cheese
¼ cup grated Parmigiano cheese
Extra virgin olive oil

Instructions

Pizza dough should be left at room temperature for at least one hour or until supple. Preheat oven to 475°. If using a pizza stone, put stone in before preheating.

When dough is supple, shape into a free-form circle that will fit onto a pizza stone or a round pizza pan. If using a stone, put a thin coating of semolina onto a long handled, wooden pizza board before placing the dough on the board. This will make it easier to slide the dough onto the hot stone. If using a round pizza pan, spread a thin layer of oil over the surface of the pan.

When dough is on either the pizza board or pan, add the four cheeses. Drizzle with extra virgin olive oil. Carefully slide the pizza onto the pizza stone, or simply put pan in the oven. Bake the pizza 20–30 minutes until dough is cooked and browned on the bottom, and cheese is melted.

Remove from oven and transfer to a cutting board. Let it rest a minute or two so the cheese can set. Slice and serve immediately.

Pizza Gorgonzola with Pine Nuts, Sun-dried Tomatoes and Fresh Chives

Pizza con Gorgonzola Pignoli Pomodori Secchi e Chives

Blue cheese may be substituted for the gorgonzola for a milder flavor.

Ingredients

1 pizza dough	1 tsp. fresh chives
¾ cup crumbled gorgonzola	extra virgin olive oil
3 Tbsp. pine nuts	fresh ground pepper to taste
½ cup sun-dried tomatoes, slivered	

Instructions

Pizza dough should be left at room temperature for at least one hour or until supple. Preheat oven to 475°. If using a pizza stone, put stone in before preheating. When dough is supple, shape into a free-form circle that will fit onto a pizza stone or a round pizza pan. If using a stone, put a thin coating of semolina onto a long handled, wooden pizza board before placing the dough on the board. This will make it easier to slide the dough onto the hot stone. If using a round pizza pan, spread a thin layer of oil over the surface of the pan.

When dough is on either the pizza board or pan, sprinkle on the cheese, and then add the pine nuts. Drizzle with extra virgin olive oil. Carefully slide the pizza onto the pizza stone, or simply put pan in the oven. Cook the pizza about ten minutes, then add the sun-dried tomatoes. Cook another 10 minutes until dough is cooked and browned on the bottom, and cheese is melted. Remove from oven and transfer to a cutting board. Sprinkle with fresh chives and fresh ground pepper. Let it rest a minute or two so the cheese can set. Slice and serve immediately.

Pizza with Oven-dried Tomatoes, Fresh Rosemary and Fontina

Pizza con Pomodori Arrostiti Rosmarino e Fontina

Ingredients

1 pizza dough
8 oven-dried tomatoes (see page 103)
1-1½ cups shredded Fontina cheese
1 tsp. fresh rosemary leaves, finely chopped
freshly ground pepper to taste

Instructions

Pizza dough should be left at room temperature for at least one hour or until supple. Preheat oven to 475°. If using a pizza stone, put stone in before preheating. When dough is supple, shape into a free-form circle that will fit onto a pizza stone or a round pizza pan. If using a stone, put a thin coating of semolina onto a long handled, wooden pizza board before placing the dough on the board. This will make it easier to slide the dough onto the hot stone. If using a round pizza pan, spread a thin layer of oil over the surface of the pan.

When dough is on either the pizza board or pan, arrange tomatoes on top of pizza, then top with the fontina and fresh rosemary. Use freshly ground pepper to taste. Carefully slide the pizza onto the pizza stone, or simply put pan in the oven. Bake the pizza 20 to 30 minutes until dough is cooked and browned on the bottom, and cheese is melted. Remove from oven and transfer to a cutting board. Let it rest a minute or two so the cheese can set. Slice and serve immediately.

PASTA

Pasta

Gnocchi in Brown-Butter Sage Sauce
Gnocchi con Burro e Salvia

This quick sauce is also great with pumpkin ravioli in the fall.

Ingredients

1½ lbs. homemade gnocchi (or frozen or fresh
      vacuum packed gnocchi)
10 large fresh sage leaves, chopped fine
1 stick butter
fresh ground pepper
fresh grated Parmigiano

Instructions

In a large pot, put gnocchi in rapidly boiling, salted water. Gnocchi are cooked when they rise to the top. Meanwhile, in a deep skillet, melt the butter on low-medium heat until browned and fragrant. (The butter must melt slowly so it doesn't burn. It should be light brown and have a nutty aroma.) Add the sage leaves and stir. Add the fresh ground pepper and stir. When gnocchi is cooked, strain well and add to sage butter sauce. Gently coat the gnocchi with the sauce. Serve with grated Parmigiano. Serves 4.

Gnocchi alla Matriciana with Pancetta and Radicchio
Gnocchi alla Matriciana con Pancetta e Radicchio Rosso

This sauce is a different take on traditional red sauce. It's a sure crowd pleaser.

Ingredients

½ stick butter
2 Tbsp. extra virgin olive oil
1 large white onion, chopped
8 thin slices of pancetta, diced
1 head of red radicchio, sliced thin

2 28-oz. cans crushed tomatoes
½ cup fresh basil, chopped
2 lbs. frozen or fresh vacuum packed gnocchi
1 cup Parmigiano Reggiano
salt and pepper to taste

Instructions

In a large sauté pan melt the butter over medium heat, and add the extra virgin olive oil. When butter is melted and oil is hot, add the chopped onion and sauté 2-3 minutes. Add the pancetta and continue to cook for several minutes until pancetta is slightly crisp. Add radicchio and let wilt. Add crushed tomatoes and basil. Stir. Add salt and pepper to taste. Bring to a boil, and continue to boil for 1 to 2 minutes. Remove from heat.

Cook gnocchi according to package directions. Add the cooked and drained gnocchi into the sauce pan and add Parmigiano Reggiano. Mix well. Spoon into bowls, and serve with additional cheese. Serves 4-6.

Goat Cheese Ravioli with aged Balsamic Vinegar and Truffle Oil

Ravioli Ripieni con Formaggio di Capra Aceto Balsamico e Olio di Tartufo

We have written this recipe for two servings because it is an expensive dish. The quality of the balsamic vinegar and truffle oil make a big difference. Use the truffle oil sparingly — a little goes a long way. This is a very simple yet elegant dish. It can be doubled if desired.

Ingredients

12 large goat cheese ravioli
6 Tbsp. good quality aged balsamic vinegar
4 tsps. good quality truffle oil
handful of fresh Italian parsley leaves, stems removed (do not chop)

Instructions

Bring a large pot of salted water to a boil. Add ravioli. Ravioli are cooked when they rise to the top. Meanwhile, in a small saucepan add balsamic vinegar and cook on low heat until reduced by almost half and the consistency is more syrupy, about 3 minutes. When ravioli is cooked, divide it between two plates. Pour the balsamic reduction over each plate of ravioli, and then carefully pour 2 tsps. of truffle oil over each. Garnish with several whole flat-leafed parsley leaves. Serves 2.

Linguini with Clams
Linguini con Vongole

Ingredients

1 ½ sticks butter
8 cloves garlic, coarsely chopped
juice of 1 fresh lemon
1 cup dry white wine
3 lbs. New Zealand Cockels
1 bunch fresh Italian parsley, chopped
1 pound dried linguini
fresh pepper to taste

Instructions

In a large pot, melt butter, being careful not to burn. Add garlic and stir. Cook on medium heat until garlic begins to bubble and becomes fragrant, 1-2 minutes, stirring frequently. Add the lemon juice and 1 cup of dry white wine. Bring to a simmer over medium high heat. Add a handful of Italian parsley and stir. Add clams that have been washed and scrubbed. Cover and simmer on medium heat about 5-7 minutes, stirring occasionally, until clams open. Discard clams that have not opened.

   Serve over linguini that has been cooked al dente, and sprinkle with additional fresh parsley and freshly ground pepper. Serves 4-6.

Orecchiette with Broccoli Pesto
Orecchiette con pesto di broccoli

This dish was an experiment that turned out to be very popular and enjoyable.

Ingredients

3 lbs. broccoli florets
½ cup pitted calamata olives
4 cloves garlic
¼ cup extra virgin olive oil
½ cup Parmigiano Reggiano, grated
¼ cup pignoli nuts
salt and pepper to taste
1 lb. orecchiette pasta

Instructions

Steam the broccoli for 10-12 minutes and then transfer to a food processor. Add the calamata olives, garlic, olive oil, pignoli nuts, salt and pepper. Blend for 2-3 minutes on high. Transfer to a large bowl and then mix in the Parmigiano Reggiano.

Bring a large pot of water to a boil, and add the orecchiette. Cook about 8 minutes or until al dente. Place the orecchiette in the bowl with the pesto and mix well. Serves 4-6.

Pappardelle with Lamb Bolognese Sauce
Pappardelle con Lamb Ragu

Ingredients

¼ cup extra virgin olive oil
4 large garlic cloves, chopped
½ cup white onion, chopped
1 large carrot, peeled and diced
2 celery stalks, diced
1 Tbsp. chopped fresh rosemary
½ cup dry white wine

1 ½ lbs. ground leg of lamb
1 ½ lbs. pappardelle pasta
2 28-oz. cans crushed tomatoes
¼ cup fresh Italian parsley, chopped
⅓ cup Locatelli cheese, grated
salt and pepper to taste

Instructions

In a 6-quart pot, heat olive oil over medium heat. Add the garlic, onions, carrots, celery and rosemary, and cook until tender, about 4-5 minutes. Add the white wine and stir. Allow alcohol to evaporate. Add the meat and brown slowly for 7-10 minutes. Add crushed tomatoes. Add salt and pepper and bring to a boil. Simmer over low/medium heat, uncovered for 30-40, minutes, stirring occasionally. When sauce is done, remove from heat and add the parsley and Locatelli cheese. Mix well.

In a separate 6–8 quart stockpot, bring water to a boil and add pappardelle. Cook pasta until tender. In a large serving bowl, add drained pasta and sauce. Spoon into individual pasta bowls and serve with additional grated cheese. Serves 4-6.

Pasta Shells, Chicken Sausage and Broccoli Rabe
Pasta con Salciccia di Pollo Arrostita e Broccoli Rape

Ingredients

2 lbs. thin chicken sausage (any flavor)
2 bunches of broccoli rabe
1 cup extra virgin olive oil
4 cloves garlic, sliced
1 medium white onion, chopped
crushed red pepper to taste

1 tsp. chicken base or 2 small
    chicken bouillon cubes, crushed
1½ lbs. medium sized pasta shells
grated Locatelli cheese for sprinkling
salt and pepper to taste

Instructions

Preheat oven to 375°. Place the sausage in a shallow roasting pan and roast for 25-30 minutes. Meanwhile, fill a 6-quart stockpot ¾ full of water and bring to a boil. Trim broccoli rabe by cutting off 2-3 inches of the stems, and boil for 10 minutes.

In an extra large frying pan, heat the olive oil and sauté the garlic, onions, and crushed red pepper over medium heat until onions and garlic are tender. When broccoli rabe is finished cooking, drain it and chop it into ½ inch pieces. Add the broccoli rabe and the chicken base or bouillon cubes to the frying pan. Cook 10-15 minutes.

In the pot used to cook the broccoli rabe, add fresh water and bring to a boil. Add the pasta and cook until al dente. Before draining the pasta, take ½ cup of pasta water and add to the frying pan. Remove sausage from the oven and cut into bite-size pieces. Add to the broccoli rabe. Drain the pasta, and then add to the broccoli rabe and sausage mixture. Sprinkle with Locatelli cheese and mix well. Add salt and pepper to taste, and then lightly drizzle with extra virgin olive oil. Serves 4-6.

Pasta with Broccoli, Garlic, Walnuts and Oil

Pasta con Broccoli Aglio Noci e Olio d'oliva

Ingredients

½ cup olive oil
1 head broccoli, cut into florets
4 cloves garlic, sliced
½ cup chopped walnuts
crushed red pepper flakes
1 lb. penne pasta
fresh ground pepper to taste
extra virgin olive oil
grated Parmigiano

Instructions

Boil salted water in a pot large enough to cook 1 lb. penne. Boil penne al dente according to directions on box. In a steamer basket set over simmering water, steam broccoli florets until bright green and still firm. While broccoli is steaming, in a deep fry pan or skillet heat olive oil. Add garlic slices and walnuts and cook over medium heat until garlic is slightly browned and walnuts are fragrant. When the broccoli is cooked, add it to the skillet and stir until broccoli is coated. Add crushed red pepper to taste. Stir.

When pasta is cooked al dente, strain, then add to broccoli mixture. Stir to coat. Serve in pasta bowls, sprinkling with freshly ground pepper and drizzling with extra virgin olive oil. Serve with grated Parmigiano. Serves 4-6.

Risotto with Wild Mushrooms, Pancetta and Peas

Risotto con Funghi di Bosco Pancetta e Piselli

Ingredients

8 thin slices pancetta
1 Tbsp. olive oil
4 Tbsp. butter, divided
1 pound mushrooms, stems removed,
    sliced (white, cremini and shiitake)
1 shallot, finely chopped
1 clove garlic, finely chopped
5 cups chicken broth

1 tsp. Italian parsley, finely chopped,
    plus extra for garnishing
1 cup frozen peas
1½ cups Arborio rice
½ cup grated Parmigiano,
    plus extra for serving
2 Tbsp. heavy cream
fresh ground pepper to taste

Instructions

In a large pot, fry pancetta as you would bacon until golden and sizzling. Drain on paper towel, let cool, crumble and set aside. In the same pot, heat the oil and 1 Tbsp. butter over medium heat. Add the sliced mushrooms and raise heat to high. Stir and cook for about 8 minutes. Remove the mushrooms and place in a bowl, covering them with foil to keep warm. In the same pot melt 2 Tbsp. butter on medium heat, and add the shallot and garlic. Cook 3-4 minutes until the shallot is softened but not browned, and the garlic is fragrant. Meanwhile, cook the frozen peas uncovered 3-4 minutes in a small dry saucepan over low/medium heat; they will release a little water. Drain and set aside.

Heat chicken broth in a large saucepan until hot. When shallots and garlic are cooked, add the rice and stir until all the grains are coated with the butter mixture. Add 1 cup of the hot stock to the pot and cook, stirring constantly, until the rice has absorbed most of the stock. Continue to cook the risotto, adding the stock 1 cup at a time, stirring constantly until all liquid is absorbed. Cook the risotto about 20 minutes until it has a creamy, porridge-like consistency. Remove the risotto from heat, and stir in the grated cheese, remaining 1 Tbsp. butter and two Tbsp. heavy cream. Stir in fresh parsley. Pour mushroom mixture over the risotto. Divide among 4 plates. Place crumbled pancetta and extra parsley over each plate. Serve immediately with fresh ground pepper and extra grating cheese. Serves 4-6.

Tubetti with Escarole, White Beans and Sweet Sausage

Tubetti con Escarola Cannellini e Salsiccia

Ingredients

2 Tbsp. olive oil
½ cup onion, finely chopped
4-6 cloves garlic, chopped
½ tsp. oregano
¼ tsp red pepper flakes
2-3 sweet sausages, out of casings and crumbled
1 head escarole, washed, dried, coarsely chopped

1 15.5 oz. cannellini beans, drained and rinsed
1 16 oz. can chicken broth
1 cup tubetti pasta
½ cup grated Parmigiano
fresh ground pepper to taste

Instructions

In a deep pot, fry sausage until browned and cooked through. Remove from pot and set aside. In the same pot, heat the olive oil on medium high. When heated, add onions and garlic and cook on medium heat about five minutes, stirring, until onions are soft.

Add oregano and red pepper flakes. Add cooked sausage. Add escarole and cook until tender, stirring, until escarole is wilted and soft. Add chicken broth and one *canful* of water. Add the beans and cook for 3-5 minutes. Bring to a boil, and then add the tubetti pasta. Cook another 5-7 minutes until pasta is cooked al dente. Gently stir in cheese and fresh pepper. Serve immediately with extra grating cheese. Serves 4.

SEAFOOD

Pesce

Chilean Sea Bass Livornese
Chilean Sea Bass alla Toscana

Ingredients

½ cup extra virgin olive oil
3 cloves fresh garlic, sliced
½ of a white onion, sliced thin
¼ lb. pitted calamata olives, cut in half
¼ lb. pitted Sicilian green olives, cut in half
2 Tbsp. large capers
¼ tsp. imported dried oregano
salt and pepper to taste
1 32-oz. can peeled crushed tomatoes
4 thick Chilean sea bass filets
½ cup chopped fresh Italian parsley

Instructions

In a large, deep frying pan, heat olive oil over medium heat. Add the garlic, onions, capers and olives and cook 3 minutes over medium heat until garlic and onions are softened. Add the crushed tomatoes. Stir. Add salt, pepper, and oregano and bring the sauce to a boil.

Reduce heat to medium-low and add sea bass filets. Cook for approximately 15-20 minutes until fish is cooked through. Do not overcook. Fish should be moist inside. Add fresh parsley and serve. Serves 4.

Chilean Sea Bass with Artichoke Hearts and Tomatoes
Chilean Sea Bass Con Carciofi e Pomodorini

Halibut may be substituted for the Chilean Sea Bass. This recipe is great to make in winter, when ripe tomatoes are very hard to find. Using canned tomatoes makes it an easy weeknight meal.

Ingredients

4 1½-2 inch wide pieces Chilean sea bass
1 14 oz. can artichoke hearts, drained
1 14 oz. can chopped tomatoes
4 shallots cut in fourths lengthwise
6 whole garlic cloves
2-3 Tbsp. olive oil

½ cup white wine
2 handfuls of fresh thyme sprigs
⅔ cup chicken broth
salt and fresh ground pepper to taste
extra virgin olive oil
fresh lemon juice

Instructions

In a large skillet, heat oil on medium high heat. When hot, add the shallots and lower heat to medium. Stir to coat and cook until starting to soften, 5-8 minutes, and then add the garlic. Stir to coat. Caramelize both until browned and fragrant, another 5-8 minutes. Add the artichoke hearts and cook a few minutes until browned. Add white wine and chicken broth. Stir, scraping up any brown bits. Add tomatoes, season with salt and pepper, then add one handful thyme sprigs. Simmer for 5 minutes on medium low heat.

Preheat oven to 350°. Spray a grill pan with an olive oil based cooking spray, and place over high heat. Rinse fish and pat dry. Season both sides with salt and pepper. Lightly pour extra virgin olive oil over both sides of fish, rubbing in the oil to coat the fish. Place fish in heated grill pan. Grill 4 minutes on each side until fish is browned. Cook fish in oven until easily flaked with a fork. Remove cooked thyme sprigs from artichoke mixture. Spoon artichokes, shallots, tomatoes, garlic and broth among 4 shallow bowls. Place fish on top of mixture. Squeeze fresh lemon juice over each piece of fish and garnish with rest of fresh thyme sprigs. Serves 4.

Basa Mediterranean
Basa Mediterranea

A favorite summer dish when tomatoes are ripe and fresh basil is plentiful.

Ingredients

6 Tbsp. olive oil
1 pint cherry tomatoes
6 cloves garlic, sliced
10 pitted calamata olives, coarsely chopped
4 basa filets or Canadian flounder
½ cup dry white wine
salt and fresh ground pepper to taste
8-10 large basil leaves, torn in pieces

Instructions

Heat oil in a skillet over medium high heat. When hot, lower heat to medium and add the garlic. Stir. Add cherry tomatoes and olives and stir again. Cook about 10 minutes, stirring occasionally. When the tomatoes begin to soften, gently use a potato masher or the back of a wooden spoon to crush each tomato. (Careful—seeds, juice or oil may splatter out of the tomatoes.) Cook another 5 minutes over medium high heat. Add wine.

Rinse fish and pat dry. Season both sides with salt and fresh ground pepper. Place fish over tomato mixture. Cook 3-5 minutes depending on thickness of fish, and then carefully turn fish over, add basil and cook another 5 minutes, making sure fish is cooked through. Divide fish among 4 plates, scooping up mixture and putting it on top of fish. This dish is especially nice with fresh steamed string beans. Serves 4.

Mussels alla Marinara
Cozze alla marinara

This dish can be served as an appetizer with toasted garlic bread, or over linguini as an entrée.

Ingredients

4 dozen mussels
2 28-oz cans peeled San Marzano tomatoes
2 Tbsp. fresh garlic, sliced
1 cup bottled clam juice
2 Tbsp. fresh chopped Italian parsley
¼ cup dry white wine
½ cup extra virgin olive oil
salt and pepper to taste

Instructions

In a large pot, heat olive oil over medium heat, and then add garlic and white wine. Sauté for 2-3 minutes. Thoroughly wash the mussels in cold water and discard any that remain open. Place mussels into pot, then add tomatoes, salt and pepper. Bring to a boil. Lower temperature to medium heat and cook 15-20 minutes until mussels are open and sauce is hot. Remove from heat and add parsley. Serves 4-6.

Pan-Seared Tuna Steaks with Peppers, Onions and Balsamic Vinegar

Tonno in Padella con Peperoni, Cipolla e Aceto Balsamico

Ingredients

4 tuna steaks
3 Tbsp. olive oil
pinch of red pepper flakes
2 cloves garlic, minced
½ each of green, yellow, and red pepper, sliced
½ large onion, sliced
several Tbsp. all-purpose flour
½ cup good quality balsamic vinegar
salt and pepper to taste

Instructions

Rinse tuna steaks and pat dry. Salt and pepper each side, and then lightly coat fish with flour, shaking off excess. In a skillet, heat oil over high heat and add red pepper flakes to season the oil. When hot, place the tuna steaks in the skillet and cook 2-3 minutes depending on thickness of steaks and how rare you like it. Turn fish over and cook another 2-3 minutes, until fish is brown on both sides. Remove from pan, set aside and keep warm with foil.

To the same skillet, add the peppers, onion and garlic. Stir and cook over medium high heat until soft, 8-10 minutes. Place tuna steaks back in skillet with the vegetables. Raise the temperature to high and slowly and carefully pour the balsamic over the fish, partially turning your face away in case the vinegar splatters. Cook on high heat 1 minute, turning fish once to coat with remaining balsamic vinegar from pan. Remove fish from pan and divide among four plates, placing vegetable mixture on top of fish and spooning any remaining balsamic vinegar. Serves 4.

Sal's Hometown Red Snapper
Sal's Dentice alla Amanteana

Ingredients

3 red snapper filets
4 Tbsp. extra virgin olive oil
12 paper-thin slices of peeled white potato
1 onion, sliced into nine thin rings
¼ lb. mixed green and calamata olives,
    pitted and chopped

1 Tbsp. chopped garlic
20 grape tomatoes cut in half
3 Tbsp. dry white wine
1 Tbsp. fresh Italian parsley, chopped
dried oregano to taste
salt and pepper to taste

Instructions

Preheat oven to 350°. Place red snapper skin side down in a shallow baking dish greased with olive oil. Lightly brush filets with olive oil. Place 4 slices of potato fanned out over each filet, and then top with 3 slices of onion.

    Mix olives, garlic, tomatoes, remainder of olive oil and white wine together, and then pour mixture over the top of filets. Sprinkle with salt, pepper, fresh parsley, and oregano. Cover and bake for 30 minutes. Uncover and bake an additional 10 minutes. Serves 4-6.

Shrimp Oreganata
Gamberi Oreganata

Ingredients

3 Tbsp. bread crumbs

3 Tbsp. extra virgin olive oil

1 Tbsp. chopped garlic

crushed red pepper to taste

1 large red onion, sliced

2 lbs. shrimp, peeled and cleaned

24 grape tomatoes, cut in half

½ cup dry white wine

salt and pepper to taste

1 tsp. dried oregano

1 Tbsp. grated Pecorino Romano cheese

1 Tbsp. fresh Italian parsley, chopped

Instructions

In a small nonstick frying pan, toast the bread crumbs for 2-3 minutes over medium heat. Set aside. In a large nonstick frying pan, heat the olive oil over medium heat, and then add the garlic, crushed red pepper and onions. Sauté over medium heat for 3 minutes.

Place shrimp and tomatoes in the pan and sauté another 2-3 minutes. Add white wine and cook an additional 10 minutes. Add salt, pepper and oregano. Stir.

Transfer the shrimp and tomato mixture to a serving platter and sprinkle with the toasted bread crumbs, cheese, and parsley. Serves 4-6.

Stuffed Roast Salmon
Salmone Ripieno al Forno

Ingredients

2 ½ lb. thicker cut salmon filet, skinless, bones removed and
     butterflied (your fishmonger can do this for you)
3 Tbsp. extra virgin olive oil, plus extra
3 cloves garlic, chopped
½ white onion, chopped
2 zucchini, chopped
¼ cup dry white wine
1 egg
2 cups seasoned bread crumbs
½ lb. Locatelli cheese, grated
1 Tbsp. chopped fresh Italian parsley
salt and pepper to taste

Instructions

Preheat oven to 350°. In a large, non-stick frying pan, heat the olive oil over medium heat. Add the garlic, onions, and zucchini and cook 3-5 minutes until tender. Add the white wine and let alcohol evaporate. Remove pan from heat. Add the bread crumbs, cheese, egg, parsley, salt and pepper. Mix well. Drizzle a little olive oil over salmon and spread stuffing mixture over the filet. Roll up tightly. Place salmon seam side down on a lightly greased baking dish. Drizzle a bit more olive oil over the salmon, and bake covered for 30 minutes. Uncover and bake an additional 10 minutes. Serves 4-6.

Stuffed Swordfish
Pesce Spada Imbottito

Ingredients

2 Tbsp. extra virgin olive oil
1 ½ Tbsp. chopped fresh garlic
1 red onion, sliced thin
⅓ lb. sun-dried tomatoes, sliced in thin strips
2 Tbsp. tomato puree
3 swordfish steaks
2 tsp. dried imported oregano
salt and pepper to taste
1 tsp. chopped fresh Italian parsley

Instructions

In a large, non-stick frying pan, heat the olive oil over medium heat, and then add the garlic, onions, and sun-dried tomatoes. Cook 3 minutes until all are softened. Add the tomato puree, stir, and cook another minute. Remove from heat.

Make a pocket in each swordfish steak and stuff with the onion, garlic, and sun-dried tomato mixture. Rub each side of steaks with olive oil, salt, pepper and dried oregano and return to the frying pan. Cook for approximately 10 minutes per side, over medium heat until fish is cooked through. Be careful not to overcook fish. It should be moist inside. Garnish with fresh parsley. Serves 4-6.

Tuna Carpaccio
Carpaccio di Tonno

Ingredients

1 baguette sliced in ¼-inch rounds
1 ½ lbs. sushi grade yellowfin tuna, sliced paper thin
⅓ cup extra virgin olive oil, plus extra
¼ lb. soft goat cheese
15 calamata olives, pitted and sliced in half
12 sun-dried tomatoes sliced thin
salt and pepper to taste
fresh chopped Italian parsley

Instructions

Preheat oven to 350°. Brush baguette slices with olive oil and lightly toast in the oven. Set aside. Lightly brush a large, flat serving platter with olive oil. Arrange the tuna slices over the olive oil. Combine the goat cheese and ⅓ cup olive oil in a mini food processor and blend. Spoon cheese mixture in small amounts over tuna. Sprinkle the sun-dried tomato slices and olives over the tuna. Salt and pepper the dish to taste, and then drizzle lightly with more extra virgin olive oil. Sprinkle with chopped parsley and serve. Serves 4-6.

POULTRY

Pollo

Chicken Breast Stuffed with Sun-dried Tomatoes and Smoked Mozzarella

Cotaletta di Pollo Ripiena con Pomodori Secchi e Mozzarella Afomicata

Ingredients

3 Tbsp. olive oil
4 large boneless chicken breasts
small container of sun-dried tomato spread
1 smoked mozzarella cheese
½ cup dry white wine
olive oil
fresh ground pepper

Instructions

Preheat oven to 350°. Rinse chicken breasts and pat dry. Cut a deep pocket lengthwise in each chicken breast, being careful not to cut all the way through. Place 2-3 heaping teaspoons of sun-dried tomato spread into each pocket. Place 1½ thin slices of smoked mozzarella into each pocket, on top of the sun-dried tomatoes. Close up pocket, pushing ingredients in. Secure with 2 toothpicks so pocket stays closed during cooking. Put a little olive oil on the bottom of a baking dish, just enough to lightly coat. Lightly coat tops of chicken breasts with olive oil. Place the four breasts in the baking dish and pour wine around chicken. Season chicken with a good amount of freshly ground pepper. Place in oven and bake for 30-40 minutes or until chicken is lightly browned and cooked through. Remove toothpicks. Serves 4.

Chicken Paillard with Arugula, Red Grape Tomatoes and Fresh Mozzarella

Cotoletta di Pollo con Arugula Pomodorini e Mozzarella Fresca

Ingredients

4 large breaded and fried chicken cutlets
balsamic-based vinaigrette dressing
3 bunches arugula, chopped
1 small fresh mozzarella, cubed into bite-sized pieces
1½ cups red grape tomatoes, cut in half

Instructions

Preheat oven to 350°. Heat breaded and fried chicken cutlets on a cookie sheet until heated through. Meanwhile, thoroughly wash and dry arugula and remove coarse stems. Chop coarsely. Combine tomatoes, arugula and cubed mozzarella with a tablespoon or two of the balsamic vinaigrette. Gently toss.

When cutlets are heated through, put on individual plates and top them with a generous amount of the arugula salad. Serve immediately. Serves 4.

Chicken Piccata
Pollo Piccata

Serve with rice and fresh steamed broccoli for a delicious meal.

Ingredients

½ stick butter
1 Tbsp. chopped garlic
2 Tbsp. flour, plus extra for dredging chicken
1 Tbsp. capers
6 thin chicken cutlets
½ cup dry white wine

2 cups chicken broth
12 white mushrooms, sliced
¼ cup freshly squeezed lemon juice
fresh ground pepper to taste
canola oil for frying
¼ cup chopped fresh Italian parsley

Instructions

Dredge chicken cutlets in flour and set aside. Heat ¼ inch of canola oil in a large frying pan until hot. Cook cutlets 2-3 minutes on each side. Remove from pan and set aside.

Clean out frying pan and melt butter. Sauté garlic, and then add flour. Mix until smooth, and then slowly add white wine, chicken broth, lemon juice, capers, mushrooms, and pepper. Stir. Return chicken to the pan and bring sauce to a low boil. Reduce down and continue to cook until sauce is slightly thick, approximately 25 minutes.

Garnish with fresh parsley. Serves 4-6.

Chicken Scarpariello with Pork Sausage

Petto di pollo scarpariello con salciccia di maiale

Ingredients

3 lbs. boneless chicken breasts
1 lb. sweet pork sausage
regular olive oil
4 Tbsp. extra virgin olive oil
2 Tbsp. fresh garlic, chopped
1 white onion, chopped
½ green bell pepper, diced
½ red bell pepper, diced

12 large crimini mushrooms, sliced
¼ cup balsamic vinegar
2 28-oz. cans crushed tomatoes
½ cup chicken broth
4 Tbsp. fresh chopped Italian parsley
crushed red pepper to taste
salt and pepper to taste
all-purpose flour for dredging

Instructions

Preheat oven to 375°. Cut chicken into 1 inch cubes. Dredge chicken in flour, shaking off excess. In a large frying pan, heat 1 to 1½ inches of regular olive oil, enough to cover bottom of pan. When oil is hot, add the chicken pieces and cook until golden brown. Drain chicken on paper towels to remove any excess oil. While chicken is cooking, put the sausage in a baking pan and bake for 20-25 minutes, turning once. Remove sausage from oven, let cool slightly, and cut into ½-inch pieces. Set aside.

To prepare the sauce, heat 4 Tbsp. extra virgin olive oil in a large pot over medium heat. Add the garlic, onions, red and green peppers and crimini mushrooms. Sauté for 3-4 minutes, then add the balsamic vinegar. Stir.

Add the cooked chicken and sausage, and cook for 2-3 minutes, mixing well. Add the chicken broth, crushed tomatoes, salt and pepper to taste and 2 Tbsp. of the freshly chopped parsley. Stir. Bring to a boil, and then simmer over medium-low heat for 35-40 minutes. Transfer to a serving bowl and sprinkle with the additional fresh parsley. Serves 4-6.

Fried Chicken Cutlets with Pecorino Cheese

Cotolette di Pollo Fritte con Formaggio Pecorino

A delicious variation on breaded chicken cutlets. Cheese is used instead of bread crumbs. Leftover chicken makes great sandwiches paired with fresh sliced tomato, oregano, extra virgin olive oil, and fresh mozzarella.

Ingredients

6 chicken cutlets
6 eggs
2 Tbsp. flour
½ cup heavy cream
2 cloves garlic, finely chopped
1 Tbsp. chopped fresh Italian parsley
fresh ground pepper to taste
1 lb. Pecorino Romano cheese, grated
canola oil for frying

Instructions

Beat 6 eggs together in a shallow bowl. Add the flour, heavy cream, garlic, chopped parsley, and pepper to the egg mixture. Mix well.

Place Pecorino Romano cheese in a shallow bowl. Dip each chicken cutlet in the egg mixture, and then press both sides into the Pecorino Romano cheese. Refrigerate chicken for 30 minutes.

In a 12-inch, non-stick frying pan, add enough canola oil to cover the entire bottom of pan. Heat the oil over medium heat. When oil is hot, fry the chicken cutlets over medium heat until chicken is browned and cooked through. (Another cooking option: lightly spray the chicken slices with olive oil and bake in the oven at 350° for 30 minutes, instead of pan frying.) Serves 4-6.

Grilled Chicken Fra Diavola alla Yvette

Petto di Pollo Arrabiatta alla Yvette

Ingredients

3 Tbsp. extra virgin olive oil
4 cloves garlic, chopped
¼ medium white onion, chopped
⅓ cup hot sliced cherry peppers

6 boneless chicken breasts
1 quart marinara sauce
salt and fresh ground pepper to taste
1 Tbsp. chopped fresh parsley

Instructions

Grill chicken on an outdoor grill or in an indoor grill pan. Spray either one you choose with an olive oil-based cooking spray so chicken will not stick. Cook chicken on both sides over medium heat until chicken is almost cooked through.

Cut grilled chicken slices into 1½-inch strips. Set aside.

In a deep, non-stick frying pan, heat olive oil, and then add the garlic, onions, and cherry peppers. Cook for 3-4 minutes over medium heat. Add the chicken strips, marinara sauce and salt and pepper. Cook 8-10 minutes until sauce is hot and chicken is cooked through. Garnish with fresh parsley. Serves 4-6.

Sal's Note: This is a spicy dish, terrific served alone or tossed with penne pasta. A dry red wine would complement it nicely. It is named after a customer who cannot eat fried food. She asked me to make a grilled version, and it's become a hit in the store.

Grilled Chicken Breasts with Marinara, Sun-dried Tomatoes and Goat Cheese

Petto di Pollo alla Griglia con salsa alla Marinara Pomodori Secchi e Formaggio di Capra

Ingredients

4 large chicken breasts
olive oil
1 small container marinara sauce
16 sun-dried tomatoes, softened, if necessary, in hot water
1 log soft goat cheese
½ cup fresh Italian parsley, chopped
salt and fresh ground pepper to taste

Instructions

Marinate chicken breasts in a ziplock bag with olive oil for about 30 minutes to an hour. Preheat oven to 350°.

Preheat to medium high heat a grill or an indoor grill pan that has been sprayed with an olive oil based cooking spray. When hot, grill the chicken breasts about 5-7 minutes per side until browned and almost cooked through. Remove from heat and set aside.

In a baking dish big enough to hold the four chicken breasts, spoon a layer of marinara sauce on the bottom. Place chicken breasts on top of sauce. Spoon remaining sauce over and around chicken breasts. Top each breast with 3-4 sun-dried tomatoes. Place two slices of goat cheese on each chicken breast, over the sun-dried tomatoes. Bake in the oven for 15-20 minutes until chicken is cooked through and cheese is bubbly and melted.

Divide chicken and sauce among four plates. Garnish with fresh chopped parsley and fresh ground pepper. Serves 4.

Chicken Pomodoro
Pollo di Pomodoro

Ingredients

4 large, thin chicken cutlets
3 Tbsp. olive oil
½ tsp. oregano
salt and pepper to taste
2 garlic cloves, coarsely chopped
¼ cup vodka

½ cup chicken broth
½ cup tomato chopped
2 tsp. heavy cream
⅓ cup scallions, green parts only, chopped fine
fresh ground pepper to taste

Instructions

Heat the olive oil in a large skillet over medium heat. Season the chicken cutlets with salt, pepper and oregano. When oil is hot add garlic. Stir. Cook for 30 seconds, and then add the cutlets to skillet. Cook on both sides until browned and cooked through. Remove chicken and set aside, keeping warm on a plate covered with foil.

Deglaze pan with the vodka. Add the chicken broth and bring to a boil. Add the heavy cream and stir. Put the chicken back in the pan. Add the tomato pieces and cook until they are heated and soft, about 1-2 minutes. Add the scallions, stir and remove from heat.

Arrange the chicken on four plates, scooping the tomato mixture on top of the cutlets. Season with freshly ground pepper. Serve with a side pasta dish or hearty salad. Serves 4.

Roasted Chicken Sausage with Potatoes, Onions and Rosemary

Salciccia di Pollo Arrostita con Patate, Cipolle, e Rosmarino

Ingredients

4 lbs. thin chicken sausage (any flavor)
4 large Idaho potatoes, peeled and cut into chunks
½ cup extra virgin olive oil, divided
6 cloves garlic, sliced
1 large white onion, sliced
1½ Tbsp. chopped fresh rosemary
1 tsp. dried oregano
½ cup dry white wine
salt and pepper to taste

Instructions

Preheat oven to 375°. Place the potato chunks in a large roasting pan, then toss with ¼ cup olive oil, salt and pepper. Bake for 25-30 minutes, and remove from oven. Cut the sausages into 2-inch pieces and add to the potatoes. Return pan to oven and cook for another 25-30 minutes.

While sausage and potatoes are cooking, heat ¼ cup olive oil in a medium-sized, non-stick frying pan over medium high heat. Add the garlic, onions, rosemary and oregano and sauté for 10 minutes until onions are lightly browned and spices are fragrant. Add the white wine to the pan and let cook for several minutes until the alcohol burns off.

Add the sautéed onion mixture to the sausage and potatoes, and mix well. Season with more salt and pepper, if desired. Serves 4-6.

Pan Sautéed Turkey Cutlets
Petto di Tacchino Passato in Padella

A quick and easy low-fat meal. Delicious with fresh steamed asparagus sprinkled with lemon juice.

Ingredients

8 thin turkey cutlets
all-purpose flour, enough to coat cutlets
2 Tbsp. dried oregano, divided in half
salt and pepper to taste
3 Tbsp. olive oil
2-3 garlic cloves, minced

juice of one fresh lemon
½ cup chicken broth
½ cup dry white wine
½ cup fresh cilantro, chopped,
               plus more for garnishing

Instructions

Combine the flour, 1 Tbsp. oregano, salt and pepper in a shallow dish. Rinse and pat dry the turkey cutlets. Dredge in the flour mixture to coat, shaking off excess. In a skillet, heat the olive oil over medium heat. When hot, add the turkey cutlets. (You may have to use two pans or do the cutlets in batches. Do not overcrowd cutlets in pan.) Brown cutlets about 3-5 minutes per side. Remove them from pan and keep them warm on a plate covered with foil.

In same pan, add the garlic, fresh lemon juice, chicken broth, wine, 1 Tbsp. oregano, and cilantro. Heat a few minutes until wine is bubbling. Put turkey cutlets back in pan to heat through. Remove cutlets and divide among four plates, pouring sauce over cutlets. Garnish with additional fresh chopped cilantro. Serves 4-6.

MEAT

Carne

Stuffed Veal Chops
Costolette Di Vitello Ripiene

Ingredients

6 center cut veal chops, 1½ inches thick
⅓ cup dried porcini mushrooms
2 Tbsp. extra virgin olive oil
3 cloves garlic, chopped
2 medium shallots, chopped
12 sun-dried tomatoes, chopped

4 thin slices Prosciutto di Parma, chopped
3 Tbsp. seasoned bread crumbs
6 slices Fontina cheese
2 Tbsp. chopped fresh Italian parsley
fresh ground pepper to taste

Instructions

Preheat oven to 375°. Soak mushrooms in a small dish of hot water for 2-3 minutes until softened. Remove and chop fine. In a medium sized frying pan, heat olive oil over medium heat. When hot, add the garlic, shallots, mushrooms, sun-dried tomatoes and prosciutto. Sauté 4-6 minutes. Remove pan from heat, and mix in the bread crumbs and ground pepper. Add a bit of olive oil if necessary; mixture should be moist.

Create a pocket in each veal chop by slicing through the center horizontally. Be careful not to cut all the way through. Fill each pocket with the stuffing mixture. In a roasting pan lightly coated with olive oil, arrange the chops and bake for 30 minutes uncovered. Remove chops from the oven and place one slice of fontina cheese on each chop. Return chops to the oven and bake for 3-5 minutes longer until cheese is melted. Garnish with fresh parsley. Serves 6.

Veal Saltimbocca
Scaloppini di Vitello Saltimbocca

This recipe is a variation of the traditional saltimbocca made with just prosciutto and fresh sage. Fontina cheese has been added for a new twist on a classic.

Ingredients

6 thin veal cutlets
Salt and pepper to taste
2 Tbsp. butter
6 slices imported prosciutto
12 fresh sage leaves, finely chopped; extra for garnish
Small chunk of Fontina cheese, cut into 12 slices
½ cup dry white wine
salt and fresh ground pepper to taste

Instructions

Salt and pepper the veal cutlets. On one half of the cutlet, place a slice of prosciutto, then sprinkle with approximately ¼ tsp. chopped sage. Place two thin slices of Fontina cheese over prosciutto and sage. Fold the plain end over the prosciutto and Fontina, and secure with a toothpick. Heat the butter in a large skillet over medium heat. When melted and hot, add the veal. Cook 3-5 minutes. Add wine to pan. Cook 2 minutes. Turn veal over and cook another 5 minutes. Remove toothpicks. Serves 4-6.

Veal Milanese
Cotolette di Vitello alla Milanese

Ingredients

6 thin veal cutlets
4 eggs
2 Tbsp. flour
¼ cup heavy cream
2 cloves garlic, chopped fine
1 Tbsp. chopped fresh Italian parsley
1 tsp. paprika

3 Tbsp. Locatelli cheese, grated
1 lb. seasoned bread crumbs
canola oil for frying
fresh ground pepper to taste

Instructions

Beat eggs together in a shallow bowl. Add the flour, heavy cream, garlic, chopped parsley, paprika, Locatelli cheese, and pepper. Mix well.

In another shallow bowl, place the breadcrumbs. Dip each veal cutlet in the egg mixture, and then into the seasoned bread crumbs. When all the cutlets are coated, refrigerate for 30 minutes.

In a large skillet, cover the bottom of the pan with canola oil. Heat the oil over medium heat. Add the veal cutlets and continue to cook over medium heat for 3-5 minutes on each side, until browned and cooked through. Serves 4-6.

Note: For a lighter version, the veal can be baked in a 350° oven for 20-30 minutes until brown and cooked through. Lightly coat a baking dish, as well as the veal cutlets, with an olive oil based cooking spray before baking.

Osso Buco a la Marsala
Osso Buco alla Marsala

This dish is a rich meat lover's delight accented with Marsala. Excellent served with a creamy risotto.

Ingredients

6 center cut veal shanks
1 stick butter
½ white onion chopped fine
2 dozen crimini mushrooms, sliced
1 cup flour for sauce, extra to dredge meat
3 Tbsp. porcini mushroom powder
1½ Tbsp. beef base, or 2 beef bouillon cubes, crushed

8 cups chicken broth
4 cups Marsala wine
½ cup chopped fresh Italian parsley
canola oil for frying
fresh ground pepper to taste

Instructions

Preheat oven to 400°. In a large stock pot, melt butter over very low heat. Add onion and sauté a few minutes. Add the flour, porcini mushroom powder and beef base or bouillon. With a wooden spoon, mix until there are no lumps. Add Marsala and chicken broth and cook over medium heat, stirring frequently, until sauce thickens. Set aside.

Dredge the veal shanks in flour and set aside. In a large frying pan, heat ½ inch of oil. Once hot, brown veal shanks 2-3 minutes per side. Set meat on paper towels to absorb excess oil. In a deep baking dish, add the veal shanks and crimini mushrooms. Cover with the sauce and then with aluminum foil and bake for 1 hour. Reduce heat to 350° and continue baking an additional hour. Remove from the oven and let stand 15 minutes before serving.

Garnish with fresh chopped parsley. Serves 4-6.

Pork Filet Pizzaiola
Filetto di maiale alla pizzaiola

Mama Aida would often serve this mouth-watering dish with penne or spaghetti, and Parmiagiano Reggiano cheese.

Ingredients

3 lb. pork filet sliced thin
1 white onion, sliced
2 Tbsp. chopped fresh garlic
1 Tbsp. oregano
4 Tbsp. extra virgin olive oil
½ cup white wine
2 28-oz. cans peeled and crushed San Marzano tomatoes
½ cup fresh chopped Italian parsley, more for garnish
hot crushed red pepper to taste
salt and pepper to taste

Instructions

In a deep, 12-inch frying pan, heat the extra virgin olive oil over medium heat. Add onion and garlic and sauté for 2-3 minutes. Add pork and brown for 4-5 minutes over medium heat. Add wine, tomatoes, oregano, fresh parsley, salt, pepper and crushed red pepper and bring to a boil. Lower temperature to medium low and cook for about 25-30 minutes. Garnish with additional parsley. Serves 4-6.

Pork Loin Roast Stuffed with Prosciutto di Parma
Arrosto di Maiale con Prosciutto di Parma

An excellent meat for holiday gatherings. Delicious with mashed potatoes and sautéed broccoli rabe.

Ingredients

4 lbs. boneless pork loin, butterflied
olive oil
2 Tbsp. chopped garlic
2 Tbsp. chopped fresh Italian parsley
salt and fresh ground pepper to taste
½ lb. grated Locatelli cheese
6 thin slices of Prosciutto di Parma
6 slices provolone cheese, domestic variety

Instructions

Preheat oven to 375°. Drizzle butterflied pork with olive oil. Layer all ingredients on top of the pork, starting with the garlic, parsley, pepper, grated Locatelli, prosciutto, and provolone. Roll up the meat and tie securely with butcher string in approximately five places around the rolled-up roast.

Sear the roast in a frying pan with olive oil to brown the outside. Transfer to a roasting pan and drizzle with a little olive oil. Sprinkle with salt and pepper. Pour 2 cups of water in pan and cover. Bake for 1 hour. Uncover and bake for an additional 10-15 minutes. Remove from oven, cover, and let stand 15 minutes before slicing. Serves 4-6.

Marinated Pork Filet with Barbeque Sauce
Filetto di Maiale marinato in salsa di "barbeque"

This delicious recipe is great with a fresh mozzarella and tomato salad or grilled mixed vegetables.

Ingredients

3 lb. pork filet
1½ cup good quality barbeque sauce
½ cup water
3 cloves garlic
½ cup fresh chopped Italian parsley
fresh ground pepper to taste

Instructions

Butterfly the pork filet or ask your butcher to do it. Place pork in a large zip-lock bag. Add barbeque sauce, water, garlic, parsley and fresh pepper. Close the bag and massage the pork filet until all ingredients are mixed and meat is coated. Marinate and refrigerate for 2-3 hours. Choose one of the following methods to cook the pork:

Barbequeing: Preheat grill to 400° for 10 minutes, then lower heat to medium. Place pork filet on barbeque and cook for 12-15 minutes on each side.

Roasting: Preheat oven to 375°. Roast pork filet in oven for 30-35 minutes.

After cooking, let meat rest on a wooden board for a few minutes so juices can be absorbed. Slice on the diagonal. Serves 4-6.

Grilled Rib Eye Steak with Mascarpone Gorgonzola Sauce

Bistecca alla Griglia con salsa di Mascarpone Gorgonzola

Ingredients

4 1½-inch-thick rib eye steaks
½ lb. Mascarpone cheese
½ lb. gorgonzola cheese
3 cloves garlic
½ cup extra virgin olive oil
fresh ground pepper to taste

Instructions

To prepare sauce, put marscarpone, gorgonzola, garlic and olive oil in a mini food processor. Process until well mixed and smooth. Preheat grill until very hot. Brush steaks with olive oil, and sprinkle with freshly ground pepper. Grill steaks to desired doneness.

Arrange steaks on large serving dish, and while steaks are hot, place a dollop of the cheese mixture on each steak. Serve immediately as cheese begins to melt. Serves 4.

Steak Marsala
Filetto di Manzo alla Marsala

A family recipe using filet mignon instead of chicken or veal. Nice to serve at an elegant dinner party.

Ingredients

4 filet mignons, ½ inch thick
salt and pepper
all-purpose flour for dredging
2 Tbsp. olive oil
1 Tbsp. butter
½ large onion, finely chopped
1 clove garlic, minced

½ cup Marsala wine
¼ beef broth
1½-2 cups sliced white mushrooms
½ cup Italian parsley, chopped,
    plus more for garnish
freshly ground pepper to taste

Instructions

Season filets with salt and pepper, then lightly dredge in flour, shaking off excess.Heat olive oil in a skillet over medium heat. When hot, add steaks and cook 2-3 minutes on each side. Remove steaks and keep warm on a plate covered with foil.

Add 1 Tbsp. butter to skillet. When melted and hot, add onion, garlic, mushrooms and parsley. Cook a few minutes until onion is soft. Add the wine and the beef broth and stir. Bring to a boil, then reduce heat and add the filets back to the pan to heat through. Serve with sauce spooned over filets. Garnish with additional chopped parsley and freshly ground pepper. Serves 4.

Filet Mignon in a Red Wine Sauce atop a Parmesan Disc with Gorgonzola Mashed Potatoes

Filetto di Manzo con Salsa di Vino Rosso Parmigiano Tostato Gorgonzola e Pure di Patate

Ingredients

4 filet mignons, 1 inch thick
salt and pepper to taste
1 Tbsp. butter, plus 4 Tbsp. cold butter for wine sauce
1 shallot, finely chopped
1 clove garlic, finely chopped
2 long, fresh thyme sprigs, plus leaves for garnish
2 cups dry red wine such as Merlot or Cabernet Sauvignon

For the Parmesan discs:
Small container imported grated
    Parmesan

For gorgonzola mashed potatoes:
See page 105

Instructions

Preheat oven to 350°. Salt and pepper filet mignons, set aside. In a small, deep sauce pan put 1 Tbsp. butter and melt on medium high heat. Add shallot and garlic and stir to coat. Cook about 1 minute, stirring occasionally. Add red wine and stir. Add the thyme sprigs. Raise heat to high, and bring to a boil. Boil until liquid is reduced by at least half, about 15 minutes, stirring occasionally. Remove from heat and run sauce through a fine sieve into another saucepan. Return the sauce to the stove and cook on low heat, adding 4 Tbsp. cold butter, one tablespoon at a time until melted, whisking continuously. Season with salt and pepper. Cover and keep warm. Make the potatoes at this point and keep warm.

For the Parmesan discs, cover a large cookie sheet with parchment paper. Place 4-5 Tbsp. of parmesan in 4 mounds, flattening a bit, on the cookie sheet. The discs will spread as they cook, so be sure to leave room between them. Bake in the oven for 12 minutes or until golden brown. Remove from oven. Let cool on cookie sheet for 1 minute; the discs will become crisp. Gently remove, and set aside.

Heat grill or indoor grill pan on high heat. Cook filet mignon to desired doneness. To plate: Pour a generous spoonful of red wine sauce onto a dish with a generous lip. Place a mound of gorgonzola mashed potatoes in center of dish. Carefully place a Parmesan disc on top of the potatoes, and then gently put filet mignon on center of disc. Top with fresh thyme leaves and serve immediately. Serves 4.

VEGETABLES

Vegetali

Broccoli, Oil and Garlic Livornese
Broccoli Aglio e olio ala Toscana

Ingredients

½ cup extra virgin olive oil
2 medium white onions, sliced
6 cloves garlic, sliced
½ lb. pitted calamata olives, sliced in half
½ cup capers
crushed red pepper to taste
3 lbs. broccoli florets
1 lb. grape tomatoes, cut in half
salt & pepper to taste

Instructions

In a large frying pan, heat olive oil over medium heat. Add onions and garlic and sauté a few minutes. Add calamata olives, capers and crushed red peppers. Stir, and continue to cook 2-3 minutes, then add broccoli, salt and pepper. Lower heat and cover. Cook for 10-15 minutes until broccoli is almost cooked. Add grape tomatoes and cook 5 more minutes. Transfer to a serving dish and drizzle with additional olive oil. Serves 4-6.

Broccoli Rabe with Olive Oil and Fresh Garlic
Broccoli Rape con Aglio e Olio

This side dish is a traditional favorite. Leftovers are terrific when tossed with sausage and pasta.

Ingredients

½ cup extra virgin olive oil
8 cloves fresh garlic, sliced
1 tsp. crushed red pepper
3 bunches broccoli rabe
salt & pepper to taste

Instructions

Fill an 8-quart stock pot with water, add a little salt and bring to a boil. Wash broccoli rabe, trim off 3 inches of stems, and coarsely chop. Add the chopped broccoli rabe to the boiling water and cook 10-15 minutes until tender. Remove from water and drain for 15 minutes in a colander.

In a large frying pan, heat olive oil over medium heat, then sauté garlic and crushed red pepper on low heat for 2-3 minutes. Add broccoli rabe to pan and continue to cook an additional 20-25 minutes covered, on low heat. Add salt and pepper to taste. Transfer to a serving dish and drizzle a bit of extra virgin olive oil on top. Serves 4-6.

Escarole and Cannellini Beans with Caramelized Onions
Escarole con Fagioli e Cipolla

This is an excellent accompaniment to any simple meat dish. It's also delicious with crusty bread.

Ingredients

½ cup extra virgin olive oil, plus extra
2 medium white onions, sliced
8 cloves garlic, crushed
crushed red pepper to taste
2 15-oz. cans cannellini beans
3 bunches fresh escarole
Salt and pepper to taste

Instructions

Fill an 8-quart stockpot with water and salt and bring to a boil. Wash escarole, remove bottom stems and coarsely chop. Cook 10-15 minutes until escarole is tender. Remove from the water and drain in a colander. Set aside.

In a large frying pan, heat the olive oil over medium heat. Add the onions, garlic and crushed red pepper. Sauté 8-10 minutes until soft. Drain and rinse the cannellini beans and add to the pan. Squeeze any excess water from escarole, and then add to the pan. Stir, and continue to cook an additional 3-5 minutes. Put in a serving dish, drizzle a bit of extra virgin olive oil over the top, and enjoy family style. Serves 4-6.

Fresh Cauliflower with Lemon Pepper
Covolifiori con lemon pepper

This dish can also be served over pasta.

Ingredients

2 heads cauliflower
2 Tbsp. extra virgin olive oil
1 stick butter
1 white onion, sliced
1 Tbsp. lemon pepper
2 Tbsp. fresh Italian parsley
Salt to taste

Instructions

Cut cauliflower into florets and place in a large pot. Add two cups of water and ½ teaspoon salt. Cover and cook for 10-12 minutes over medium heat. When cooked, drain cauliflower and place in a large bowl.

In a skillet, melt the stick of butter with 2 Tbsp. of olive oil. Add the onions and sauté for about 10 minutes until the onions are soft. Pour over the cauliflower, and then add the fresh parsley, lemon pepper and salt. Mix well. Serves 4-6.

Oven Dried Tomatoes
Pomidori al Forno

This method sweetens plum tomatoes, to use as a garnish or as an ingredient in various dishes.

Ingredients

4-5 plum tomatoes, sliced in half
extra virgin olive oil, for sprinkling
1-2 large cloves of garlic, chopped fine
Kosher salt
freshly ground pepper

Instructions

Preheat oven to 350°. Arrange tomatoes on a baking sheet, face up. Sprinkle the chopped garlic, Kosher salt and freshly ground pepper onto the tomatoes, and drizzle them with olive oil. Bake for one hour.

Gorgonzola Zucchini
Zucchini al Forno con Gorgonzola

Blue cheese can be substituted for a milder flavor.

Ingredients

1-2 medium sized zucchini, diagonally sliced into ¼-inch slices
8 oz. crumbled gorgonzola
fresh ground pepper
olive oil

Instructions

Preheat oven to 350°. Lightly oil a baking dish which will also be your serving vessel. Arrange two to three overlapping rows of zucchini slices in the dish. Sprinkle zucchini with crumbled gorgonzola, then sprinkle fresh ground pepper to taste. Bake for about 25 minutes until zucchini is softened and cheese is almost melted. Switch oven to broil. Broil on high heat a minute or two until cheese is golden brown and bubbly. Keep oven door open slightly when broiling, and watch constantly. The cheese will brown very quickly. Remove from oven. Serves 4.

Gorgonzola Mashed Potatoes
Gorgonzola e Pure di Patate

Ingredients

3-4 large baking potatoes
3 Tbsp. butter
milk
salt and pepper to taste
1 cup crumbled gorgonzola

Instructions

Peel and quarter the potatoes, place in medium size pot and cover with cold water. Bring to a boil, reduce heat and cook until soft. Drain off all the water. Add the butter and enough milk to make a creamy consistency. Be careful when adding the milk, pouring in a little at a time, mixing with a hand-held mixer, and then adding more milk if needed. The potatoes should not be runny. When the right consistency is reached, add the gorgonzola and mix again until thoroughly combined and melted. Season with salt and pepper to taste. Makes 4-6 servings.

Roasted Garlic Mashed Potatoes

Pure di Patate con Aglio Arrostito

Ingredients

3-4 large baking potatoes
1 large bulb garlic
3 Tbsp. butter
milk
salt and pepper to taste
extra virgin olive oil

Instructions

Preheat oven to 350°. Carefully slice off the top of a large garlic bulb, exposing the tops of the cloves. Remove any loose papery skin. Salt and pepper the bulb, then pour a little stream of olive oil over cloves. Wrap bulb loosely in foil and bake in the oven for one hour.

When slightly cooled, remove each clove from the bulb with the point of a knife. The cloves should be very soft and browned, and they should come out easily. Mash in a small bowl and set aside.

Prepare mashed potatoes in the usual way. When potatoes are soft and cooked, strain and put back into pot. Add the butter and enough milk to make a creamy consistency. Be careful when adding the milk, pouring in a little at a time, mixing with a hand-held mixer, and then adding more milk if needed. The potatoes should not be runny. When the right consistency is reached, add the roasted garlic and mix again until thoroughly combined. Season with salt and pepper to taste and serve. Makes 4-6 servings.

Rocco's Baked Eggplant with Gorgonzola

Melanzane e Gorgonzola al Forno di Rocco

Sal's Note: A flavorful side dish my brother Rocco came up with. It's a nice variation of eggplant parmigiana. You can also serve this over pasta.

Ingredients

3 large eggplants, peeled and cut into ¾-inch cubes
3 medium white onions, chopped
6 Tbsp. chopped fresh garlic
2 slices bacon, chopped
12 medium to large white mushrooms with stems, chopped
1 lb. crumbled gorgonzola cheese (reserve ½ cup for topping)
½ lb. Locatelli Romano cheese, grated

½ cup extra virgin olive oil
1 bag fresh baby spinach
½ tsp. fresh ground pepper

Instructions

Preheat oven to 350°. In a large frying pan, heat olive oil over medium heat. Sauté the onions and garlic for a few minutes. Add the bacon and sauté until slightly crisp. Add the mushrooms and eggplant. Mix well and cook until eggplant and mushrooms are tender. Add the spinach and both cheeses (not including reserved ½ cup gorgonzola). Mix well, then transfer to a shallow baking dish. Sprinkle reserved cheese on top and bake for 5-10 minutes until cheese is melted. Serves 4-6.

Sauteed Peas with Mushrooms, Onions and Pancetta
Piselli soffritti con Funghi, Cipolla, e Pancetta

This is an excellent side dish for roasted meats. Especially good for the holidays.

Ingredients

2 lbs. frozen peas
⅓ lb. pancetta, chopped
½ cup extra virgin olive oil, plus extra
1 medium white onion, sliced thin
4 cloves fresh garlic, sliced
1 lb. crimini mushrooms, sliced
1 Tbsp. chopped fresh Italian parsley
1 Tbsp. Locatelli cheese, grated
salt and pepper to taste

Instructions

Place frozen peas in a large, non-stick frying pan (with no water) and cook over low heat for 10 minutes, stirring as they release the frozen water. Add olive oil, onions and garlic to the pan, and cook 5-7 minutes. Add the sliced mushrooms and cook for another 10 minutes, stirring. Remove the pan from the heat.

In a small frying pan, slowly cook the pancetta over low heat until crisp. Sprinkle the crisped pancetta over the peas, and then sprinkle the fresh parsley and Locatelli cheese. Add salt and pepper to taste. Place peas in a serving bowl and drizzle a bit of extra virgin olive oil on top. Enjoy family style. Serves 4-6.

Zucchini Provençal
Zucchini di Provincia

Ingredients

3 cloves garlic, finely chopped
½ large onion, cut into thin strips
3 medium zucchini, sliced ¼-inch thick, diagonally
5 plum tomatoes, chopped
3 Tbsp. olive oil
½ cup dry white wine
1 tsp. dry oregano
¼ tsp. crushed red pepper flakes
salt and fresh ground pepper to taste

Instructions

In a large deep skillet, heat the olive oil on medium high heat. When hot, add the onions and sauté, stirring occasionally for 5 minutes. Add chopped garlic and stir. Cook until onions are softened, about 5 minutes. Add chopped tomatoes and stir. Cook 5 minutes.

Add zucchini and red pepper flakes and cook uncovered on medium heat for 20 minutes. Add white wine and dry oregano and cook 10 minutes over medium high heat. Salt and pepper to taste. Makes 4-6 servings.

DESSERTS

Dolci

Biscotti with Almonds and Mini Chocolate Chips

Biscotti alla Mandorla con Cioccolatini

Ingredients

¾ cup whole almonds
3 large eggs
1 tsp. vanilla
¼ tsp. pure almond extract
1 tsp. baking soda

2 cups all-purpose flour
¾ cup sugar
dash of salt
½ cup mini chocolate chips

Instructions

Preheat oven to 350°. Place nuts on a cookie sheet and bake in oven for 8-10 minutes. Let cool. Lower oven temperature to 300°. In a small bowl beat the eggs, vanilla and almond extract with a wire whisk. In a large bowl, combine the flour, sugar, baking soda and salt. Add the egg mixture and mix until blended. Slice the nuts into halves or thirds and add to the mixture, and then add the mini chocolate chips. Gently mix. Divide the dough in half.

Grease and flour a baking sheet. Form dough into two logs about 1½ inches wide and 8 inches long. Space them on the baking sheet at least 2 inches apart. Bake in the middle of the oven for 50 minutes or until golden brown. Transfer to a cooling rack, let cool 5 minutes, and then place on a cutting board. Using a serrated knife, slice the cookies diagonally about ½ inch thick. Lay the slices back on the baking sheet, flat side down. Bake 12 minutes, then turn cookies over and bake another 12 minutes. Store in an airtight container. Makes about 3 dozen.

Chocolate Torrone with Toasted Peanuts

Torrone di Cioccolato con Nocciole

Ingredients

2 lbs. dark chocolate, coarsely chopped
or broken into pieces
1 Tbsp. canola oil
1 lb. toasted unsalted peanuts
2 Tbsp. brandy
8 x 8 disposable foil tray

Instructions

Preheat oven to 350°. Create a double boiler by placing a 6-quart pot over an 8-quart pot filled halfway with boiling water. In the 6-quart pot, add the dark chocolate and canola oil, and immediately turn down heat. Simmer, and let chocolate melt slowly.

Meanwhile, spread the peanuts evenly on a baking sheet. Toast in the oven for about 10 minutes. making sure they do not burn. Add the peanuts to the melted chocolate, mix well and remove from heat. Stir in brandy and pour chocolate mixture into a disposable foil tray. Refrigerate for an hour, uncovered, until hardened. Cut into chunks and enjoy. Serves 4-6.

Crepes Nutella
Tramenzini di Nutella

Ingredients

1 ½ cups all-purpose white flour
2 cups milk
1 egg
1 tsp. vanilla

1 stick butter with paper still on
1 medium jar Nutella chocolate spread
powdered sugar for garnish
fresh strawberries (optional)

Instructions

In a large bowl, mix the flour, milk, egg, and vanilla by hand with a whisk until batter is smooth. Heat a small crepe pan on medium heat. Peel down the waxed paper on the stick of butter halfway so you can use it to hold the butter while working. Take the stick of butter and glide across the entire bottom of the crepe pan to lightly coat. Then take a ladle and spoon in about a ¼ cup of batter into the crepe pan. Swirl the pan so the batter coats the bottom evenly. Cook about 2 minutes, then carefully flip the crepe to the other side or use a spatula to turn. Cook another 2 minutes. Crepes should be lightly browned on both sides. Set them aside on a plate as you go.

Continue until all the batter has been used. Let cool. To stuff the crepes, take 1-2 Tbsp. of Nutella and cover half of each crepe, leaving room around the sides. Fold the plain end over the half with the Nutella. You now have a half moon. Fold in half again. Arrange crepes on individual plates or on a platter. Garnish with powdered sugar and fresh strawberries, if desired. Serve at room temperature. Makes about a dozen crepes.

Grilled Panini with Nutella and Bananas
Panini alla griglia con Nutella e Banana

This is a delicious snack that children love to eat and enjoy helping to make. Terrific at a birthday party or as a treat on a play date.

Ingredients

2 loaves French baguette
1 medium jar Nutella chocolate spread
1 bunch of bananas

Instructions

Divide baguettes by cutting them into 4 equal pieces. Slice each section lengthwise. Place face down on a panini press or toast in a 350° oven until warm and slightly toasted. Nutella should be at room temperature. Spread Nutella generously on both sides of each section of baguette. Slice bananas on the diagonal, ¼ inch thick. Arrange over one side of the nutella covered bread. Close each section, and then press together to set. Serves 6-8.

Limoncello Truffles

A unique and original dessert created for Limoncello lovers!

Ingredients

14 oz. box of almond biscotti, crushed
1 cup toasted pignoli nuts, crushed
2 cups of confectioners sugar

½ cup of imported Limoncello liquor
9 oz. melted dark chocolate
2 Tbsp. canola oil

Instructions

Lightly toast pignoli nuts for 5-10 minutes in 300° oven and let cool. Place dark chocolate and canola oil in a 6 quart pot, then place over an 8 quart pot of water filled halfway to create a double boiler. Bring water to a boil, then immediately turn down heat. Let chocolate melt slowly. Stir. Turn off heat.

Place nuts in food processor and lightly crush, making sure the crushed amount equals one cup. Transfer to a stainless steel bowl. Add biscotti to the food processor and process for 30 seconds until biscotti are crushed fine.

Transfer the crushed biscotti to the bowl with the nuts, then add the sugar, Limoncello and melted chocolate. Mix well by hand. Moisten hands with a small amount of canola oil to prevent sticking when making the truffle balls. Roll the mixture into small, 1 inch balls, and then place in a single layer on a serving dish. Refrigerate for at least 1 hour to set, then remove and set at room temperature for 1 hour before serving. Makes approximately 2 dozen.

Strawberry Zabaglione
Zabaglione con Fragole

Ingredients

6 egg yolks at room temperature
¼ Marsala wine
½ cup confectioner's sugar
1 pint strawberries, washed, dried and chopped
    (save a few whole strawberries for garnish)

Instructions

Create a double boiler, but do not allow top pot to be submerged in the water from the bottom pot. Gently simmer water in bottom pot. Put eggs, Marsala and sugar in top pot, then place over simmering water. With a hand-held mixer using a whisk attachment, whisk egg mixture at medium speed for 8 minutes in the double boiler. Mixture will become frothy, creamy and smooth and will be pale yellow in color. Cool slightly.

Place the chopped strawberries in two large glasses or four small glasses. Pour zabaglione into the glasses covering the strawberries. Serve warm. Serves 2 to 4.

Pignoli Cookie Sandwich with Cannoli Cream

Pignoli biscotti inbottiti con crema di cannoli

These delicious cookies are unique because they combines two popular Italian desserts. Serve with a frozen shot of Limoncello, and it will be a dessert your friends and family will never forget.

Ingredients

1 lb. dry Impastata ricotta
1 cup powdered sugar
¼ cup Amaretto liquor
½ cup mini chocolate chips (optional)
1 tsp. orange zest
1 lb. pignoli cookies

Instructions

Place the dry Impastata ricotta in a large bowl. Add sugar, Amaretto and orange zest, and hand mix for 2-3 minutes until all ingredients come together. Add the mini chocolate chips and stir to combine.

Using a spoon, put a good amount of Cannoli cream on one pignoli cookie and place another cookie on top to make a sandwich. When all the cream is used up and the cookies are made, place on a dish and refrigerate. When ready to serve, sprinkle some powdered sugar on top. Makes about 20 cookies.

Amaretti Cookies with Toasted Almonds and White Chocolate

Biscotti Amaretti Cioccolata Bianca alla Mandorla

Ingredients

2 lbs. white chocolate
2 Tbsp. canola oil
1 lb. whole almonds, toasted

1 14-oz. bag Amaretti cookies, crushed
2 Tbsp. unsweetened cocoa powder
3 Tbsp. Amaretto liqueur

Instructions

Preheat oven to 350°. Place almonds on a cookie sheet and toast in the oven about 10 minutes or until fragrant. Be careful not to burn. While almonds are toasting, create a double boiler by placing a 6-quart pot over an 8-quart pot filled halfway with boiling water. In the 6-quart pot, add the white chocolate and canola oil, and immediately turn down heat. Simmer, and let chocolate melt slowly. Stir.

Turn off heat once the chocolate is melted, but keep on top of double boiler. Add the toasted almonds, crushed Amaretti cookies and cocoa powder to the melted white chocolate. Stir in the Amaretto liqueur, and mix until thoroughly combined. Place foil over a large cookie sheet. Spoon mixture, a tablespoon at a time, onto the foil. Refrigerate for at least an hour until cookies are hard. Remove and bring to room temperature before serving. Makes approximately 2 dozen.

Momma's Miniature Cheesecake Cups

Tortine di Formaggio della Mamma

Kerriann's note: My mother made these often during my childhood. They're a great dessert for a party, and make a wonderful presentation. You will need miniature muffin tins for this recipe.

Ingredients

For the graham cracker crust:
1 ¼ cups graham cracker crumbs
5 Tbsp. melted butter
¼ cup sugar

For the topping:
1 can cherry pie filling
1 can blueberry pie filling
1 can crushed pineapple

For the filling:
1 pound cream cheese
4 eggs
1 tsp. vanilla
½ cup sugar

Instructions

Preheat oven to 350°. Line mini-muffin tins with paper or foil cups. Mix ingredients for graham cracker crust in a small bowl. You will have crumbs left over. Put ½ tsp of graham cracker crust into the foil-lined pans. Blend filling ingredients in a blender until smooth. Pour into the tiny cups and bake in the oven for 10-12 minutes until the tops are dry. Remove cheesecakes from tins and cool slightly.

For the topping, place one cherry in the middle of a mini cheesecake, then place 3 small blueberries in the middle of another, and then place a small teaspoonful of pineapple on another. Continue process until you have even amounts of each. Chill in refrigerator at least an hour. Filling can be made the day before and chilled. Toppings should go on the day of the party for the best presentation. Makes 60.

Tiramisu

Ingredients

1 lb. Marscarpone cheese, room temperature
1 egg
1 cup granulated sugar
⅓ cup Amaretto liqueur

1 ½ cups cold espresso coffee
1 14-oz. package lady finger cookies
⅓ cup cocoa powder
1 cup dark chocolate shavings

Instructions

Place Marscarpone cheese in a shallow mixing bowl. Separate the egg yolk and egg white; add yolk to marscarpone cheese, set aside egg white. Add sugar to egg yolk and Marscarpone and mix with a handheld mixer until well combined. In a separate bowl, whip the egg white with the mixer on high speed until foamy, 1-2 minutes. Add egg white and Amaretto to Marscarpone mixture and mix for 3 minutes.

Place the cold espresso in a shallow bowl. Dip half of the lady fingers quickly in the espresso, then line the bottom of an 8 x 10 glass or china baking dish with the dipped lady fingers. After the first layer, spread half of the Marscarpone mixture over the lady fingers. Sprinkle with half of the cocoa powder. Repeat process, adding the remaining espresso-dipped lady fingers and Marscarpone to form another layer. Sprinkle with the remaining cocoa and finish with shaved chocolate.

Refrigerate overnight. This dessert can be made up to two days ahead, or it can be prepared and frozen for later use. Serves 4-6.

The backstories
behind these recipes and
those who created them ...

THE BALDANZA STORY

The creed that Wendell Willkie lived by stated in part, "I believe in America because in it we are free — because we have great dreams and because we have the opportunity to make those dreams come true."

This philosophy has drawn millions of people, since the founding of our country, to emigrate to our shores. Whether it is to find work, or to create a better way of life, people from all over the world have come here in hopes of obtaining a piece of "the American Dream."

This cookbook is not just about the food. It is about the dream that led up to the delicious creations — the remarkable story of the Baldanza family, and one man's journey into the unknown to seek a better life.

Nicola (Sal) Baldanza was born to Aida and Francesco Baldanza in the small coastal village

Twins Rocco and Sal at their first holy communion

of Amantea, Calabria, Italy in 1961. Sal grew up in a modest home with three brothers and four sisters. From oldest to youngest, they were Anna, Silvana, Alberto, Franca, the twins Rocco and Sal, Antonella and Giuseppe.

Aida spent her days raising the children and cooking, while Francesco earned a living as a fisherman. The Baldanzas enjoyed life in their small community, where everyone knew everyone else. In 1976, however, their security ended when Francesco died unexpectedly at forty-eight. What the family thought had been a long bout with a stomach virus turned out to be terminal stomach cancer. Following two surgeries, Francesco passed away only three months after being diagnosed, leaving Aida with eight children ranging in age from three to twenty-two.

Life for the Baldanzas changed dramatically. Aida had always wanted her children to finish school, but now money was needed for food and clothing. The twins, Sal and Rocco, had to work full time instead of going to high school. They had been working after school since they were seven, gathering the wood needed to make wooden crates that carried oranges and other fruits to market. Now they were employed to build the crates.

Aida was a strong woman and kept her family together despite the hardships of losing a husband after twenty-five years. "She was a tough woman, and still is," Sal recalls. "She was tough with us, too … a lot of wooden spoons," He laughed. "She could get through anything. She always did what was needed without complaining, and she always pointed us in the right direction."

When they reached eighteen, Sal and Rocco received their Navy papers in the mail. They were now required to serve. This was a serious problem, because besides the twins, the only other working family member was Alberto. The Baldanzas could not afford to lose two boys to the Italian Navy. They met with some government officials and explained that the family desperately needed money. The only thing that could be done was that when one brother was finished with his eighteen-month term, the other brother would then have to leave and serve.

Rocco and Sal would be separated for three years. As their mother taught them, you do what you have to do. Sal decided to go first, so in August of 1981 he packed his bags and went to Taranto in Puglia, on the other side of the Adriatic Sea. After serving there, Sal was transferred to Rome for three months, and then to Sicily. Sicily was only two hours from home, so he could go back to visit the family every two weeks.

When Sal's term was up, Rocco, who now had a job doing construction, went into the Navy as agreed. Just a few months later, however, Sal packed his bags again and left to find new opportunities in America. There had been no work to be found for Sal in Italy, and it was time for him start a new life.

At age twenty-two, Sal didn't speak a word of English. When he arrived in the States in 1983, he would meet his sister Silvana, who had come to Huntington with her husband Vinnie during the 1970's. That would be all the family Sal would have here, and he lived with them for ten years.

Sal in the Italian Navy

The day after he arrived in this country he had a job, thanks to a few friends who had already made the journey from Italy to find work. Sal began as a dishwasher at Nina's Family Style Restaurant, then located in Huntington's Southdown Shopping Center. He worked full time, earning $125 a week. Eventually it was at Nina's where Sal would meet the sweet seventeen-year-old American girl, Kate Ebert, who bussed tables there. Kate later would become his wife.

"It was an interesting relationship," Sal recalls, "since I didn't speak much English and she didn't speak any Italian. We'd go to the movies on a date, and I'd fall asleep because I didn't know what they were saying!"

Sal was a diligent worker. During slow times he'd stay in the kitchen and watch the chef. He took a keen interest in the cooking. After a year, Nina's owner, seeing this interest, said to Sal, "I think next week you're going to start to cook. I can see you like it."

Sal went from $125 a week as a dishwasher to $250 a week in the kitchen. By 1984, with a year of cooking under his belt, Sal heard that DiRaimo's was looking for someone in their kitchen. They were paying $500 a week. Sal applied for the job and got it. At about the same time, Rocco had finished serving in the Italian Navy and made plans to come to the United States. Sal was able to get him a job at DiRaimo's, and the twin brothers were finally reunited.

Shortly after, in 1986, Alberto and youngest brother Giuseppe (Joe) now fifteen years old, arrived in Huntington and began working at the A&S Pork Stores: Joe in the Huntington store and Alberto in the Port Jefferson store. During his time in Port Jefferson, Alberto began learning how to make fresh mozzarella and other Italian specialties which would be the basis for Mr. Sausage in years to come.

After some time, Sal and Rocco grew tired of the long hours at DiRaimo's, and they approached the owners of A&S. As luck would have it, they had openings at both stores, so Sal began working with Joe in Huntington and Rocco started working with Alberto in Port Jefferson.

After six months, Joe saw an ad in *Newsday* and learned that a place called "Mr. Sausage" was available. He said to his brother, "Sal, there's a pork store in Hicksville for sale."

Sal answered, "Yeah? So what?"

Joe replied, "Let's go see."

"We didn't even know where Hicksville was!" Sal recalls. "We had no experience, we didn't know how to cut meat or how to talk with the customers. We were still learning the language!"

They went to see it anyway. The store sold only sausage and braciole, no cold cuts, cheeses or anything else you'd see in Mr. Sausage today. They thought about it for a few days when the owner approached them with a $10,000 check in his hand — someone else had made him an offer.

"I remember Joe saying to me, 'Let's get it, let's get it! We could put our money together.'" The brothers pooled all of their savings and purchased Mr. Sausage.

"I said to Joe, if we make it, we make it. If we don't, we start all over again," Sal remembers.

The original Mr. Sausage had been located at the old Farmer's Market in Hicksville during the 1960's. Grumman's was close by, and business was very good. Eventually the Farmer's Market caught fire, and the owner of Mr. Sausage had to find a storefront, which he did, only a mile or so away. But a year and a half after moving there, the owner had put his store on the market. He was older, and running the store had become too much for him. It was at this time that Joe had happened to see the ad.

"So we have this store now," Sal recalls. "It was me, Joe, Alberto, Rocco and my brother-in-law Vinnie. What do we do now? Alberto was the only one making the mozzarella, and we did a little bit of cooking — not that much, because back then people did their own cooking. But we put a lot of money into the business, and started doing well. Of course, Grumman was there. Thousands of people were working close by, so we were very busy. Eighteen months later, though, Grumman began laying people off. We got scared, so we decided to look for an addi-tional place in case we started losing customers — plus we were five people working in the same store."

"We found this place in Copiague for about $1,200 a month. Most rents were $3-4,000, so $1,200 was good. We bought the store for $50,000 because we had made some money in the Hicksville store. We stayed for two years, but the store never grew. We didn't have enough experience. Also, the clientele was looking for more of a deli-type environment, and we didn't have that. So two years later we got rid of the store and we lost $50,000." Sal pauses. "We went back to Hicksville … everybody … and we started all over again."

"We all lived in Huntington, but nobody knew Mr. Sausage there. We used to go to this little place in Halesite … at the time it was called Salerno's Deli. We did some business with them, bringing dried and fresh sausage that they bought from us. I could see their store wasn't doing so good. It was empty all the time, so I said to my brother, 'Why don't we give him some money, cash, and we'll take the place. I think this is a good area.' And my brother Alberto says, 'What, are you crazy?'"

"I kept telling my brothers, I know the guy's not doing good. He's going to close … he's going to close. But nobody (the brothers) wanted to do it."

Shortly thereafter, they received word from a salesman that the Salerno had closed. The owner of the store wanted someone in there with experience, hoping the business would be around for a while. He visited the brothers at the Hicksville store and decided that they were the only ones who could possibly make it in the Halesite location. He saw they had experience and he liked what they were doing. He asked $23,000 for the store.

"We put all our money together again, but we came up short," Sal explains. "We had just lost $50,000 in the Copiague store. We didn't have that kind of money. What were we going to do? I told my brothers, we've got to get that store." He continues, "I was only married to Kate a year at this point. Kate told her mother about the problem. She asked me, 'How much do you need?' I told her we're short about $12,000. She said, 'I'll give it to you because I believe in you guys. If you make money, you pay me back. If you don't make the money, it's water under the bridge.'" Sal laughs, recalling the moment. "She also said she'd pay for our advertising. So we have the money now — and nobody wants to buy the store. Rocco, Joe, Albert, my brother-in-law … they didn't want to buy it because they were scared, and I understood why. They said if we didn't make it, then what were we going to do?"

Mama Aida making some of her delicious dishes in the kitchen of their home in Amantea

"I also had a bunch of people I knew at the time saying 'don't do it, don't do it.' I listened to that but I said, you know what? I'm going to do it by myself. We've been in business for five years. This is what we're doing. We've got to take this last chance. If we don't make it over here, everybody is going to do something else … a mechanic, somebody will do this, somebody will do that. I just think we have to take this opportunity now. They still said no, we don't want the store. I tried to have some friends convince them. Finally, after a lot of talking we were all in agreement. Joe had agreed to come with me to manage it. So we bought the store and we started working. We did everything ourselves. We were making sausage, we were cooking, we were mopping the floor, we were washing dishes … everything."

For months, Sal and Joe ran the store with no help of any kind. It wasn't until that Christmas they hired one guy to work the front counter. Six or seven months later, the store started growing. By the time they left that location eight years later, they had seven people working for them. Now, in their present location on Union Place they have fourteen working for them, and twenty-five during the Christmas season. Since they began in Halesite, the business has tripled.

"Making the decision to go with it opened the door for everybody. We got through the hard times. As the Calabrese say, 'testa dura.' You've got to think it, you've got to believe it, don't give up!" Sal says.

"We knew our products were good, we just had to believe we could make it. We really took a chance coming to Huntington. Nobody knew Mr. Sausage. We had to bring the people in. We only advertised for six months. That's it. We never advertised again."

In 2004 they closed the Hicksville store and opened up another store in Melville which is run by Rocco, Alberto and their brother-in-law Vinnie. It is here where their famous sopressata (a dried Italian sausage) is made. They learned how to make it on their own. A friend gave them the basics, but it has taken years to perfect it. The Baldanzas have been making sopressata for sixteen years now, and they feel that they have perfected it in the last eight years. Five to six hundred pounds are made each week by Alberto. It takes about four weeks to dry out. It is sold in the store as well as to restaurants and delis.

As for the prepared food in both stores, Sal knew that consistency in the taste and quality of the food was critical to the success of the business. He held fast to his roots and his Italian heritage. He says that some of his recipes were discovered through trial and error, others were researched, and of course most were family-inspired.

Alberto (l.) and Joe (r.)
making sausages

"Mama Aida's Sauce" is a traditional recipe from the countryside where Sal grew up, and is a sauce his mother cooked often during his childhood. Made from fresh vegetables from local growers, Sal adapted this family favorite to honor his mother. It's now a staple in the store.

"Nicolas Sauce" was named after Sal's first child. Sal was looking for healthy, quality food that would appeal to kids. This mild red sauce loaded with homemade chicken mini-meatballs has become a favorite of many customers and their children.

Sal enjoys creativity in cooking, and his products and food are both unique and diverse. He describes his food as rustic and simple, and made with fresh ingredients with a southern Italian influence. Sal is constantly developing new recipes and often asks customers to sample them. Anyone who has gone to Mr. Sausage knows that it always smells fantastic there. Something is always being cooked, and large platters of delicious food are lined up creatively along the overstuffed countertops. "Seeing and smelling the food right there makes you want to buy it on the spot," one regular customer states. "It's fresh, it's homemade. When I come in I rarely leave with just one item. Everything looks so good you just want to try it all. It's like coming home. It's definitely a dangerous place to come to if you're hungry," he laughs.

It's this kind of "homey" feeling that the customers keep coming back for. "Everyone is like family here," says Sal. "Our store isn't a chain. It's a family-run business with an intimate atmosphere. I'm interested in getting to know my customers and their families. I love people and I enjoy making them happy. "

Whatever Sal is doing, it's working, because customers flock to the store. Generally, Sal and his brothers put in an 80-plus-hour work week, and that's just during normal business days.

"Christmas is unique, as it is the busiest holiday of the year for us," Sal says. "An enormous amount of overtime is required and we implement a unique strategy to handle the extreme volume of business in a short period of time. During Christmas, we generally put in at least 110 hours that week." Sal explains that organization is key, and family members are critical to help with the setup and distribution of orders during Christmas. "Our family and friends will aid in this extended setup, as well as tasks like dishwashing, chopping, slicing and dicing."

Business is consistently brisk during the entire summer season, as well as on Super Bowl Sunday, New Year's, Easter, Memorial Day, the 4th of July and Labor Day. According to Sal, these are the busiest times of the year.

Rocco slicing Alberto's homemade sopressata

People come to Mr. Sausage not only for their prepared foods and hospitality, but for their prime meats, imported products, and Italian favorites such as fresh mozzarella, fresh and dried sausage and salami, which are made on the premises. The imported goods come from distributors that deal with products coming directly from Italy. Sal tries to carry exclusive items and more obscure brands and products. Basically, you can find anything Italian at Mr. Sausage.

As far as the family is concerned, Sal is happily married to Kate and enjoys their two young children, Nicolas and Olivia, and he works side by side with his brothers every day. "My brothers and I have a high respect for one another and what we each bring to the business," says Sal. "Outside of the store we socialize frequently, enjoy each other's children, and share many laughs." They also remain in constant contact with their mother in Italy, as well as other relatives who support their success in this country.

When asked what a typical day in the kitchen is like, Sal responds, "Jovial! It's a busy environment but always with laughter. A great team is very important in any business and we have that." He continues, "It's difficult at times, but overall it is very rewarding … I love my job! It's a way to reach out to others and share my love of food and people."

Sal's future goals include possibly opening more stores, or even a restaurant, and exploring other avenues that bring people and food together. "I've developed a diverse network of friends through my shop, including business owners of other trades, as well as foodies that offer great advice and have a passion for good food," he says. "My friends and family give me inspiration and have provided me with a lot of encouragement and support."

One man's journey into the unknown has become an "everyman's" success story. Was it worth the risks? As he comes out of the kitchen carrying a steaming pot of pasta fagioli, Sal says with a grin, "You bet!"

KERRIANN FLANAGAN BROSKY:
ITALIAN BRANCHES ON THE FAMILY TREE

Some may ask, "How can an author, photographer, and well-known investigator of Long Island ghost stories — with an Irish-Polish last name — possibly be co-writing an *Italian cookbook*?" What many people don't know is that Kerriann Flanagan Brosky has strong Italian roots and years' worth of cooking and entertaining under her belt.

Born and raised on Long Island, Kerriann is the oldest of three children born to Deanna and Michael Flanagan. Michael came from a big, Irish family and was the oldest of nine children. Family meals were simple and basic, and the children helped their mother peel huge buckets of potatoes and other vegetables that were stored in the root cellar.

Ernest D'Amato at the Latin Quarter

Kerriann's mother Deanna, however, came from quite a different background. Born Deanna Marie D'Amato, she is the younger of two sisters in a family of entertainers. Her mother Esmé (Kerriann's grandmother), was born and raised in England, where she became a dancer and contortionist. Deanna's father, Ernest D'Amato, although born in the United States, had roots in two Italian families. His mother was born and raised in Palermo, while his father was born and raised in Rome. Ernest met and married Esmé while he was touring Europe as the manager of Toto the Beloved Clown. The two came to America, where Ernest (known as Ernie) became the stage manager at the famous Latin Quarter in New York City. He worked side by side with Lou Walters, Barbara Walters' father. When Ernie wasn't working he did what he loved best … he cooked.

"My mother remembers as a child sitting at the dinner table for hours on Sundays," says Kerriann. "The whole family got together for a weekly feast. My great-grandmother spoke only Italian and did so much cooking, which is how my grandfather learned to cook. Thursday and Sunday were always 'gravy' days, according to my mother. Those were the days when they would make the sauce."

"My grandfather died when I was ten, but I still recall him cooking and bringing warm, fresh mozzarella to my house. His favorite things to make were homemade pizzas. I've inherited that love from him. Friday night is homemade pizza night at our house. I've taken regular pizza to new levels."

The D'Amato family would dine at the Latin Quarter and other New York City restaurants. Deanna and her sister Verona, also a dancer, acquired a love of fine food at an early age. When Deanna got married, she brought her love of cooking into the relationship, emulating her father.

Grandpa D'Amato making pizza at home, 1957

Husband Michael was thrown into a world that featured fine foods and wine, and lots of it.

Kerriann with her grandpa

"Food was a part of everything we did," Kerriann recalls. "There was always something on the stove or in the oven. All my friends wanted to eat dinner at my house. That's what my mother loved and still does. The more people she could feed the better. She'd also have extravagant sit-down dinners for friends. She really knows how to entertain."

She continues, "As we got older, if anyone had a problem that needed to be worked out, it would happen in the kitchen over a glass of wine. Everything would always take place in the kitchen. Within seconds, my mother could have an antipasto put together just with leftovers from the refrigerator."

Some say that Kerriann is a clone of her mother, who taught her how to cook. Kerriann cooks almost every night and uses only the freshest ingredients. She drives to Greenlawn to buy her eggs, and has milk delivered to her house weekly from a dairy in upstate New York.

Her two young boys are already connoisseurs, eating such things as gorgonzola, mussels, all kinds of fish and meats, and goat cheese. They are fascinated by their mother's cooking and often ask to help her in the kitchen, which she gladly allows.

"It's important to me that my children know and appreciate food," says Kerriann. "I've always kept them on a healthy, well balanced diet, and I let them try everything. Even when they were infants, I would prepare homemade baby food. When they got a little older, I'd mix some fresh garlic and spices into their food. They couldn't get enough of it. To this day, they still love garlic and they eat a ton of it. It's great because it keeps them healthy."

Kerriann's husband Karl, who introduced her to German food, considers himself very fortunate to have a wife who loves to cook. He

Deanna (l.) with Chef Gustavo Graciano and Kerriann during his cooking class

also takes pride in Kerriann's "menu board" which comes out each Friday. Since they were married sixteen years ago, she has been writing out the week's dinners on a chalkboard. It's quite a conversation piece among their friends, whose mouths water at what they read.

"I've had three books published, but sometimes I think people will remember me more for the menu board," Kerriann laughs. "Karl loved to brag about it to co-workers, and when some people didn't believe there really was one, he took a photo of it and brought it to work! Actually, the menu board makes things easier for me," she continues. "It does take a lot of planning, but this way I know what we're having every night and I can have all the ingredients I need ready for the week. I keep a list of which days I have to shop for what. I'm constantly running for fresh vegetables, meats and fish. It has to be fresh! Summer is a great season because I grow my own herbs. It doesn't get better than that, and I love to grill. The grill is an extension of my kitchen. I cook everything on it … even Friday night pizzas."

Kerriann with sons Ryan (l.) and Patrick (r.), both budding chefs

Over the years Karl has learned enough cooking from his wife to be referred to as "the sous chef." Kerriann says, "Karl and I work so well together in the kitchen, especially if we're having a dinner party. He knows how food should look and taste and how it should be presented."

Besides learning from her mother, Kerriann has taken many cooking classes through the years with professional chefs, and also teaches herself through cookbooks, magazines and cooking shows. Kerriann has over 120 cookbooks and five cooking magazine subscriptions. She has cooked everything from Italian to French, Thai, German, Irish, Cajun and Southern specialties.

"My true love will always be Italian cooking, though. For me, it's like coming home. It's pure comfort food." She continues, "If I weren't a photographer and a writer, I probably would have gone to culinary school to be a chef. I have a first cousin on my father's side who graduated from the Culinary Institute in upstate New York. She's talented and successful, and I love talking food with her." It is Kerriann's passion for cooking that led her to do this cookbook with Sal Baldanza of Mr. Sausage.

"My family and Mr. Sausage go way back to when the Baldanzas bought the Hicksville store," Kerriann recalls. "My mother was looking to find a place close by where she could buy Italian specialties. She first found this at the old Farmer's Market in Hicksville. I remember going there as a child and riding the giant merry-go-round, and smelling all the sausages being cooked. After the Farmer's Market burned down, my mother discovered Mr. Sausage and soon became one of their best customers. She would get everything she needed there."

Kerriann continues, "About a year or so after Karl and I were married, I was over in Halesite and saw that a new store had opened, called Mr. Sausage. Sure enough, when I went inside, there were the Baldanza brothers! I called my mother and said, 'You'll never believe this … we have a Mr. Sausage in Huntington!' They had just opened a few days prior. They had hardly anything in the store yet, and I remember them making me a sandwich. I told them to give it (the store) time. I knew it would work. It's been amazing for me to see the store transformed.

They started out so small and worked so hard, and it's been great to watch them grow. It's all about the food and the way they treat everyone like family."

Kerriann quickly became a regular customer. Sal and Joe began to notice what items she was buying and would routinely ask her what she was making. They were intrigued by what she devising with their products. She was putting her own spin on Italian cooking.

Sal saw her potential and would often suggest that they do a cookbook together. "He and I would joke about it, but I didn't realize how serious he was," Kerriann says. "Sal was busy with his store; I was busy with my family and my writing … where would we find the time to do a cookbook, and how?

"Sometime during the summer of 2006, my husband came home from one of his 'extended stays' at Mr. Sausage and told me that Sal had brought up the cookbook idea again. Karl told me I'd be crazy not to take him up on it," Kerriann recalls.

"I thought I must be crazy to even consider it. My third book, *Ghosts of Long Island: Stories of the Paranormal,* was due out shortly, and I had a hectic schedule of book signings, lectures and television appearances ahead of me. I had established myself as a local historian, a writer and a black-and-white photographer. Would people take me seriously if I did a joint cookbook project with Sal? But the response I got from people was amazing. Everyone was all for it, especially those I've cooked for. So I said to myself, 'Why not?' It would be challenging, that's for sure. I have spent long hours on my feet cooking as well as photographing. It had been a long time since I'd done studio-type photography, let alone food photography. The first thing I did was to buy a professional digital camera. It was a big step, having shot with film and a manual camera for twenty years. Now I had the added pressure of having to learn how to work this new camera. But looking back, I couldn't have done the photographs for this book with any other camera. I was really pleased with the results."

Throughout her life, Kerriann has gotten used to taking chances and accepting challenges. "The most difficult thing I had to deal with during my four years at C.W. Post was being a photography major. Because it wasn't a 'typical' field let alone a 'practical' one, I heard all sorts of predictions … 'You'll never get a job, you'll never make any money, it's too competitive.' Some of my friends' parents would even ask *my* parents why they would allow such a thing. But my mother and father taught me some valuable lessons … to always believe in yourself, to work hard, to never give up and to do what makes you happy. I've followed their advice. There have been many roadblocks and challenges over the years, but I've learned from them and persevered. Most of all, I love every bit of what I do, and that's more than I can say for many people I know who have taken a more conservative career route."

"I've always dreamed big," Kerriann continues. "So here was an opportunity for me to do something else I really love to do … cook. And I could share my recipes and love of cooking with everyone. To be a part of a project like this with Sal is wonderful. I couldn't imagine doing it with anyone else. We truly love food and we have a lot of fun together. Sal and his brothers are so talented. It's been a pleasure and a privilege to have cooked with them."

Another ambition of Kerriann's is to learn Italian, which she has been studying for the past several years. "It's a beautiful language," she says, "and what better place to practice than at Mr. Sausage? They're patient with me when I make mistakes. I feel that if I can cook Italian, I should be able to speak Italian, too."

Index